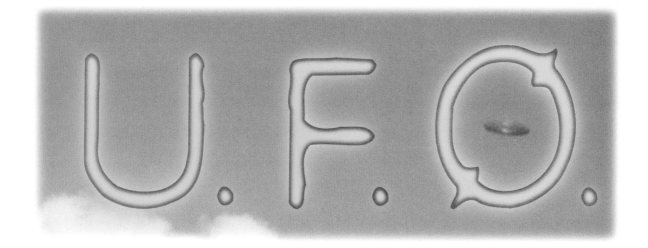

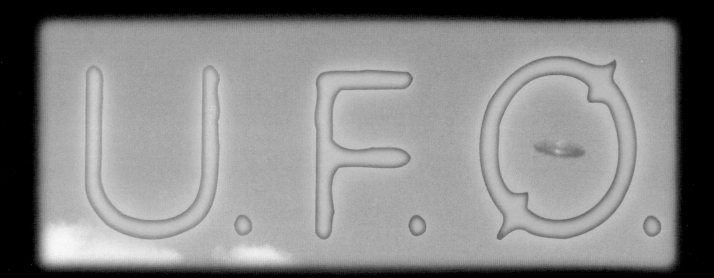

U.F.O.

EVALUATING THE EVIDENCE

Bill Yenne

S SMITHMARK
PUBLISHERS

a division of U.S. Media Holdings, Inc.
115 West 18th Street, New York, NY 10011

Editorial Consultant: Jay Olstad

Acknowledgements
The publisher would like to thank the following individuals for their assistance in the preparation of this book: Robin Langley Sommer and Barbara Paulding Thrasher, editors; Nicola J. Gillies, editorial assistant; Charles Ziga, art director; Christopher Todd Berlingo and Wendy J. Ciaccia, graphic designers; Gail Janensch and Veronica Langley for editorial advice.

The photographs and artwork for this book were researched by the author, and the author and publisher acknowledge the following individuals and institutions for permission to reproduce them here. If any error or omission has occurred in the credits below, the publisher will be pleased to correct them for future editions. Unless listed separately below, all photographs are reproduced by courtesy of the National Archives (including those from the U.S. Air Force Project Blue Book files).

Collection of Bill Yenne: 16, 18, 19, 20–21, 23 (both), 31, 34, 36–37b, 41, 45, 50, 82, 83, 100, 101, 143, 146, 156, 157; © **Bill Yenne:** 25, 37t, 40, 43, 61, 148; © **M.J. McPike:** 26; © **Jay Olstad:** 14, 97 (both), 130; © **Chris Peterson:** 71, 80, 81; **Corbis-Bettmann:** 29, 89; **Hannah McRoberts/Fortean Picture Library:** 139; **Library of Congress:** 17t, 33, 87; **Saraband Image Library:** 15, 17b; **NASA:** 58, 122, 123; **University of Manchester:** 88 (photographed by Mike Koiston) **UPI/Corbis-Bettmann:** 30, 39, 46–47, 53, 63, 65, 68, 76, 77, 106, 108, 128, 132.

This edition published in 1997 by SMITHMARK Publishers, a division of US Media Holdings, Inc., 115 West 18th Street, New York, NY 10011.

SMITHMARK books are available for bulk purchase for sales, promotion, and premium use. For details, write or call the manager of special sales, SMITHMARK Publishers, 115 West 18th Street, New York, NY 10011.

ISBN: 0-7651-9402-3

Printed in China

10 9 8 7 6 5 4 3 2 1

This book is dedicated to the scientists and researchers around the world who continue in their efforts to add to our understanding of unexplained phenomena.

Contents

Introduction

"I can assure you that flying saucers, given that they exist, are not constructed by any power on Earth."

—President Harry S. Truman,
Press conference, Washington, D.C., April 4, 1950

Throughout human history there has been an underlying fascination with mysterious natural and psychological phenomena. Early humans were mystified by fire and lightning, until these mysteries had been explored and understood. One by one, mysteries succumb to scientific explanation. A good allegory for this is contained in Mark Twain's *A Connecticut Yankee in King Arthur's Court*. A smug, scientifically literate, nineteenth-century Yankee bewilders scientifically naive medieval Englishmen with his prediction of an eclipse, a natural phenomenon which they fear because they have no basis for an explanation.

Yet for all their scientific literacy, nineteenth century Yankees eagerly gathered around tables for Spiritualist séances, and they had a voracious appetite for ghost stories.

In the twentieth century, particularly in the two decades after World War II, there was a strong belief that humans, having cracked the mystery of the atom, were on the threshold of achieving a scientific explanation for all mysteries. We all love a mystery, but we like to have the explanation on the last page.

U.F.O. EVALUATING THE EVIDENCE

Previous pages:
A Swiss woodcut (shown here in the original negative block), depicting unusual events in the sky (1566). Nicolaus Copernicus demonstrates his revolutionary 1543 model of the solar system, the first to place the Sun at its center.

Below: *A nebula in the "Local Cluster" of the Milky Way galaxy—bearing a distinct resemblance to a saucer.*

In the last half of the twentieth century, there has been a strong fascination with unidentified flying objects, which are literally objects in the sky which cannot be readily identified by their observers. In very many cases, these objects are in fact identifiable, even if not by every observer. Most of the time the objects turn out to be clouds, balloons, stars, planets, atmospheric disturbances, or airplane lights observed at unusual angles.

However, there have been events in which the objects could not—and cannot—be identified. They have defied explanation for half a century, and this has only served to deepen their mystery. It has also deepened our craving for an explanation.

In 1947, a man named Kenneth Arnold dubbed them "flying saucers" because that was what they looked like, and the media seized on that appellation. Four years later, U.S. Air Force Captain Edward Ruppelt applied the term "Unidentified Flying Object" during Project Grudge, and the crisp government acronym "UFO" became part of popular culture.

There is no final answer to the UFO riddle, but there are clues. In any good mystery story, what is left unsaid or undiscerned often tells as much as what is said and done. In the course of evaluating the evidence in UFO incidents and events, governments, especially the United States government, have left an

interesting trail of clues in what has not been asked, and what has been left undone. Why, for example, were only microfilms of the Project Blue Book files turned over to the National Archives? Where are the original files? If the U.S. Air Force no longer has them, what hap-pened to them on their way to the National Archives?

From the history of the evaluation of UFO evidence, it is quite clear that various governments, particularly that of the United States, were once very serious about identifying the unidentified.

Above: The window reflections of two interior lights—not *flying objects*—caught on film in a simple fake.

U.F.O. EVALUATING THE EVIDENCE

Right: *Twentieth-century scientists have probed the mysteries of the primary units of matter and the building blocks of organic life (on Earth, at least). Sophisticated computer models help to represent these concepts: above, a classically conceived atom with electrons orbiting the nucleus; below, a simplified DNA coil. Many have speculated that top-secret genetic research has been conducted on extra-terrestrial corpses.*

A UFO can sometimes be defined as something seen in the sky (or on land, but thought to be capable of flight) which sufficiently perplexed an observer that he made a report of it to police, to government officials, to the press, or perhaps to a private organization devoted to the evaluation of such objects. Defined in this way, there is no question as to the existence of UFOs, because UFO reports exist in fairly large numbers, and the stimulus for each report is, by this definition, literally an unidentified flying object. This UFO definition includes both delusions and insincere reports.

Before "flying saucer" and "UFO" entered the world's lexicon, most unidentified aerial phenomena that had been recorded tended to be explained as hallucinations, optical illusions (such as mirages) or as poorly observed or poorly understood natural phenomena, including ball lightning, unusually shaped clouds, meteor showers, objects carried aloft by high winds, the planet Venus, luminous swamp gas, fireflies, and will-o'-the-wisp or "sub-suns" (the brilliant reflection of light on patches of airborne ice crystals). All such phenomena still existed in the post-1947 world, but added to them were newer aerial objects, such as large weather balloons, helicopters and new models of aircraft.

With so many things in the sky prompting people's imaginations, the pastime of speculating about UFOs quickly developed a legion of followers cut from the same cloth as those who in years past had kept alive the legends of ghosts and sea monsters. Psychologists have written that some people believe in sightings of such phenomena because they want them to exist.

There has been a great deal of speculation and numerous theories about what UFOs are and who put them in the sky, and entire cottage industries have sprung up around the various theories. Most of these theories center on the theme that UFOs are of extraterrestrial origin and that they are piloted by beings from other worlds with intelligence superior to our own. In 1995, Nick Pope, one of the top UFO investigators in Britain's Ministry of Defence, announced officially that he believed they are!

Paralleling the speculation about the nature of UFOs has been the suggestion, even belief, that the United States government actually captured extraterrestrial flying saucers and has had their crews, or the bodies of deceased crew members, in secret captivity since 1947. The location was rumored during the 1960s to be "Hangar 13" (or occasionally "Hangar 18") at Wright-Patterson Air Force Base (AFB) in Ohio. In the 1990s, UFO enthusiasts came to believe that the extraterrestrials were being kept at "Area 51," a secret military facility on the Nellis AFB gunnery range south of remote highway 375 in southern Nevada. The popular 1996 film *Independence Day* portrayed a fictional "Area 51" as the location of a captured UFO and its deceased crew.

If the existence of the Lockheed F-117 and Northrop B-2 stealth aircraft was concealed—or at least obscured—by denial through most of the 1980s, then why are we expected to believe denials of the existence of "Area 51," when unconfirmed airfields from Groom Lake to Tonopah are well known to exist throughout the Nellis AFB range in the Nevada desert?

Just as the belief in a government cover-up generally parallels a discussion of UFOs, the cover-up theory is accompanied by rumors that persons attempting to pierce the veil of secrecy are dealt with harshly by government agents. One intriguing aspect of this fear of the government and its agents are the strange "Men in Black." For aficionados of UFO conspiracy theories, particularly those involving U.S. government cover-ups, the Men in Black represent a disturbing and elusive icon. According to popular UFO folklore, Men in Black appear shortly after a UFO sighting to "dissuade" witnesses from saying too much to the press. Early mentions of them

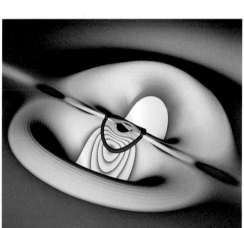

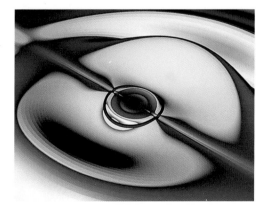

Left: *State-of-the-art computer-aided research in cosmology: this sequence simulates stages in the formation of a "black hole," a region in space in which huge gravitational forces prevent the escape of matter across its boundary, or "event horizon." UFOs, it would seem, should be a less daunting challenge for scientists than this.*

U.F.O. EVALUATING THE EVIDENCE

Right: *An era of widespread speculation about U.S. government conspiracy and concealment began with the controversy surrounding the 1963 assassination of President John F. Kennedy.*

in print include the October 1953 issue of a flying saucer publication called *Space Review*, edited by Albert Bender, and in Gray Barker's 1956 book *They Knew Too Much About Flying Saucers.*

Who they are has always been open to speculation. According to the stories, they often identify themselves as agents of the CIA, the FBI, or other federal intelligence and law enforcement agencies, possibly including the Defense Intelligence Agency (DIA) or the Air Force Office of Special Investigations (AFOSI).

While they were originally seen as nothing more sinister than American intelligence agents, some researchers have attached metaphysical meanings to the Men in Black, linking them to medieval witchcraft, the Elizabethan "Black Men," and various occult "secret societies." Despite their lack of expression and character, the Men in Black are often credited with frightening and intimidating those whom they interview. While this

strange, dark side of the cover-up theory resembles 1940s or early 1950s film noir, it has been resurrected in the popular 1990s television series *The X Files*, where all the villains seem to be Men in Black or their clandestine associates.

The view that the government has actually captured extraterrestrial craft and has their crews in secret captivity is also considered by some to be an all-but-confirmed fact. Others dismiss the rumors as nothing more than "fantastic nonsense." This is based on the theory that it would be impossible to keep a secret of such enormity for nearly half a century, and that no useful purpose would be served by engaging in such an alleged conspiracy of silence. Some people believe that the U.S. Air Force has nothing to do with UFOs, and that this super-secret matter is in the hands of the CIA or some other clandestine organization.

Many people have seen objects in the sky that they could not identify, and nearly everyone has an opinion about UFOs and the hypothesis that they are of extraterrestrial origin. This book does not catalogue every report of a UFO sighting, or every alleged visit from strange creatures with big eyes or Men in Black. It is a chronicle both of the important sightings that have occurred through the years, and of the official efforts to both evaluate and explain the evidence from these sightings. In the course of examining these sightings and the subsequent analysis of available evidence in each case, the best evaluation methods—of both physical characteristics of objects and events, and psycho-

logical study of the witnesses—are described as fully as possible. A technical appendix explains many of the key issues addressed by investigators.

A history not only of sightings, but of official investigations, this book is organized into two parallel groups of case studies. First, the case studies of the UFO reports, and second, the case studies of official evaluations. With the latter, it is of particular interest to note which elements were chosen for official evaluation, along with the evidence upon which the conclusions were based. Because of the emphasis placed in this book on evaluation and assessment techniques and criteria, this history concentrates primarily on U.S. sightings and investigations: the U.S. government has, more than any other country, both investigated UFOs widely and (usually some time later) declassified much of the official information and explanation. Where possible, reports and evaluations from other countries are included; regrettably, however, much official interpretation remains withheld from public record around the world.

Many of the reports selected for inclusion here are those witnessed by aviation and military personnel, since their training and experience minimize the likelihood of their misidentifying natural phenomena. Others are included precisely because they were proven unreliable, and the evidence upon which the object was identified is in itself of interest.

With both sightings and evaluations, there are few answers, and many unresolved questions. Perhaps by looking at UFOs through the eyes of professional investigators, some light can be shed, some pattern traced. To paraphrase the words with which Rod Serling introduced episodes of *The Twilight Zone,* the following is "submitted for your consideration."

Left: "LBJ," President Lyndon B. Johnson, was Kennedy's successor, serving until January 1969. His term of office was marred by public mistrust about information concerning U.S. involvement in Vietnam that was withheld.

Left: Public confidence in governmental integrity reached an all-time low during the 1974 impeachment hearings over the Watergate scandal, prompting Richard Nixon's resignation.

1: UFOs Before "Flying Saucers"

"I have absolutely no idea where the UFOs come from or how they are operated, but after 10 years of research, I know they are something from outside our atmosphere."

—Dr.James E. McDonald
Professor of Atmospheric Physics, University of Arizona, 1967

It took the Kenneth Arnold sighting to coin the term and to put "flying saucers" on the front pages of the world's newspapers, and Captain Edward Ruppelt's crisp military acronym to put the term "UFO" into the lexicon, but the whole notion of mysterious aerial phenomena has preoccupied humankind for centuries.

Ancient stone discs and stone spheres of unknown purpose still exist from Costa Rica to the Middle East. Are they simply some form of utilitarian millstone, or are they attempts by ancient societies to record or pay tribute to a visitation by flying objects of these shapes? In the Bible, some say the prophet Ezekiel describes a UFO in four verses (3–7) of his first book, when he recalls a "great cloud, and a fire infolding itself, and a brightness was about it."

Other ancient references are also interpreted by some "flying saucer" enthusiasts as UFO reports, perhaps the oldest one being a papyrus written during the reign of Egyptian Pharaoh Thutmose III (1504–1450 BC). Discovered by Professor Alberto Tulli, formerly director of the Egyptian Museum at the Vatican and translated by Prince Boris de Rachewiltz, it states that there was:

a circle of fire that was coming from the sky…It had no head, and the

Opposite: *Ancient stone spheres in Costa Rica are frequently cited as possible evidence of early extraterrestrial visitors.*

Below: *The remarkable technological achievements of ancient Egypt prompted Erich von Däniken's speculation that extraterrestrial intelligence may have been involved. This image from the* Book of the Dead *depicts a sun-god worshipper; many early civilizations credited heavenly bodies with supernatural powers over humankind.*

U.F.O. EVALUATING THE EVIDENCE

Right: Until the Middle Ages, any being or object in flight was regarded as possessing supernatural powers. Here, medieval sorcerers cause strange events in the skies as they summon the forces of good against the evil. The first known design for a viable flying machine was Leonardo da Vinci's famous toy helicopter, sketched in his notebooks as the sixteenth century dawned.

breath of its mouth had a foul odor. Its body was one rod long and one rod wide....Their bellies became confused through it: then they laid themselves on their bellies....They went to the Pharaoh, to report it....As his Majesty ordered...it has been examined...as to all which is written in the papyrus rolls of the House of Life. His Majesty was meditating on what happened. Now after some days had passed, these things became more numerous in the sky than ever. They shone more in the sky than the brightness of the sun, and extended to the limits of the four supports of the heavens.... Powerful was the position of the fire circles. The army of the Pharaoh looked on with him in their midst....Thereupon these fire circles ascended higher in the sky.

When Thutmose ordered the object to be examined, it was the first time in recorded history that an official evaluation of evidence was undertaken. In the second half of the twentieth century, governments would issue scores of such directives, though not all of them would be preserved so carefully for posterity.

Ezekiel's account, written about 900 years after Thutmose's, is similar to the Thutmose manuscript, and it has been suggested that the prophet knew and adapted the Thutmose story, rather than witnessing the famous fiery wheels. Both accounts are food for thought, but inconclusive, for neither Thutmose's scribes nor Ezekiel were trained in the observation of aerial phenomena.

In the third century BC there are many accounts in the Mediterranean region of "altars" or other glowing objects in the sky along with men in white clothing. During the halcyon days of the Roman Empire there were also many similar reports. Objects were observed in the vicinity of Arpi, 180 Roman miles east of Rome, that were "like

Above: *A medieval astronomer taking navigational measurements. Significant advances in astronomy were first achieved during the sixteenth century by Copernicus, Tycho Brahe, Johannes Kepler and Galileo Galilei.*

Left: *Copernicus's 1543 sketch of his solar system, showing the orbital paths of the known planets and moons.*

Above: *The link between flying and the supernatural is illustrated in this visionlike 1775 engraving of an airship and its "worshippers," as seen by Louis Guillaume de la Follie.*

west." In AD 776 , there were two objects observed near Sigisburg, Germany, in which Saxons defending a castle "beheld the likeness of two large shields, reddish in color, in motion flaming above the church...."

In 1270, an aerial vehicle allegedly became entangled in a church steeple at Bristol, England. People stoned to death the passenger who came down to free the craft. They then burned "the demon's body." Carl Gustav Jung, the famous psychologist, discovered manuscripts dating from 1561 to 1566 that contain accounts wherein people in Nuremberg, Germany, observed red, blue and black balls and circular discs in large numbers near the rising sun. They "appeared to fall to the ground as if it was all on fire and everything was consumed amid a great haze."

A 1561 woodcut in the Wickiana Collection at the Zurich Central Library shows globes with portholes along their edges. Many such images appear in manuscripts and paintings of the era. One has only to look at the late-fifteenth-century work of Hieronymus Bosch to see depictions of fanciful life-forms tumbling through the sky.

In July 1686, the German astronomer Gottfried Kirch saw a round, glowing object with a tail in Leipzig, Germany. It hovered for about eight minutes. Kirch described its diameter as half that of the moon, and said it radiated so strongly that he could read by its light until it gradually disappeared. People in nearby Schlazius also saw the object, observing that it seemed about 30 miles high in the sky and darted downward.

ships...were seen in the sky." Near Apulia, "A round shield was seen in the sky." In 170 BC, at Lanupium on the Appian Way, 16 miles from Rome, a "remarkable spectacle of a fleet of ships were seen in the air."

The historian Pliny the Younger writes that "In the consulship of Lucius Valerius and Gaius Valerius [about 100 BC] a burning shield scattering sparks ran across the sky at sunset from east to

On August 18, 1783, Tiberius Cavallo saw an oblong cloud over Windsor Castle, near London, with a glowing object just below it. It was round, brightly lit and remained stationary. It was bluish in color and it intensified gradually before moving away, splitting into two. With the sound of an explosion, it disappeared.

Lights and/or objects in the sky were reported throughout the nineteenth century, culminating with the "great airship" that was observed by many people across the United States between November 1896 and April 1897, and which has never been fully explained.

According to the March 1904 issue of *Weather Review*, the ship USS *Supply* reported having observed lights which:

appeared beneath the clouds, their color a rather bright red. As they approached the ship they appeared to soar, passing above the broken clouds. After rising above the clouds they appeared to be moving directly away from the Earth. The largest had an apparent area of about six suns. It was egg-shaped, the larger end forward. The second was about twice the size of the sun, and the third, about the size of the sun. Their near approach to the surface and the subsequent flight away from the surface appeared to be most remarkable. That they did come below the clouds and soar instead of continuing their southeasterly course is also certain. The lights were in sight for over two minutes and were carefully observed by three people whose accounts agree as to details.

Among the most widely reported UFOs in the first half of the twentieth century were those observed by American combat pilots over Germany from late 1944 through the end of World War II. These objects were variously described as semi-transparent "crystal" balls emitting red, gold, white and/or orange hues, or as balls of fire that raced along with their aircraft. They were called "feuerballs," or "kraut balls," but most often they were called "foo fighters," paraphrasing the

Below: *The Francisco Lanz airship of 1670: a somewhat "low-tech" affair, but a modest advance, nevertheless, in the history of controlled flight.*

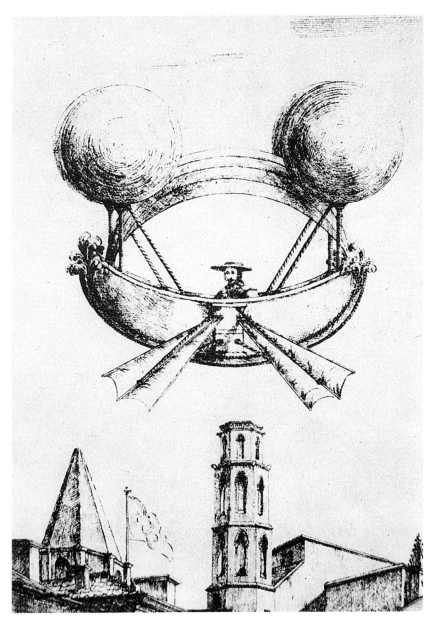

Right: An airborne photographer captured this classic foo fighter UFO (foreground, below the propellor) in August 1943 over Shreveport, Louisiana. The brightly glowing spherical object is moving along a path that is parallel with the aircraft's.

line in the Smokey Stover comic strip "Where there's *foo* there's fire."

On January 2, 1945, *The New York Herald Tribune* reported that:

On December 13, 1944, newspapermen were told that the Germans had thrown silvery balls into the air against day raiders. Pilots then reported that they had seen these balls, both individually and in clusters, during forays over the Rhine.... Pilots have been encountering this eerie weapon for more than a month in their night flights. No one apparently knows what this sky weapon is. The balls of fire appear suddenly and accompany the planes for miles. They seem to be radio-controlled from the ground, and manage to keep up with planes, flying at 300 miles an hour, so official intelligence reports reveal.

The foo fighters were never fully explained, and there is likely no single explanation. Pilots at first thought that they were German secret weapons. This may indeed have been true, but the fact that they were also observed in the Pacific Theater indicates that at least *some* of them were ball lightning, or some sort of weather phenomena.

Regarding foo fighters, former NASA staffer Dr. Richard Haines has observed that: "It is interesting to note that there have been no known official United States government technical reports published on this phenomenon although they occurred during World War II, when every enemy weapon system was carefully analyzed in order to design and build a countermeasure system."

In August 1942, also during World War II, U.S. Navy personnel observed a dozen "disc-shaped objects" flying over Tulagi Island in the South Pacific. They were at first thought to be Japanese aircraft, but their sound was reported to be a roar rather than the sound of airplane engines.

Also in the South Pacific during World War II, a U.S. Army Air Forces (USAAF) Seventh Air Force/VII Bomber Command after-action report designated 11-327 and dated May 2, 1945, notes that the crew of a B-24 bomber observed two airborne objects at their 11,000-foot altitude changing from cherry red to orange, and a white light that would die out and then become cherry red again. These objects flew parallel to the aircraft through all types of evasive action. The B-24 took a course for Guam, and one of the pursuers dropped off after accompanying the aircraft for an hour. The other continued to follow, never approaching closer than 1,000 yards, and speeding up when the B-24 went through the clouds to emerge on the other side ahead of the B-24.

A year after the war's end, another aerial phenomenon was observed in European skies. Beginning in May 1946, there were numerous reports of streaks of light in the skies over Sweden. Identified in press reports by the fanciful appellation "ghost rockets," they were seen throughout the summer. There was speculation that they may have been secret weapons launched by the Soviets who had, a year earlier, captured the German A-4 (V-2) test facility at Peenemunde on the Baltic coast, less than 100 miles from southern Sweden. Speculation was further enlivened when General Jimmy Doolittle (USAAF, retired) arrived in Stockholm in the midst of this spate of sightings on what was officially explained as unrelated, private business. The reports abated after August, when an official Swedish defense establishment inquiry failed to determine the source of the streaks

Right: On the upper right of this low-resolution photograph is a glowing object that appeared to track a flight over Richmond, Indiana, in 1954.

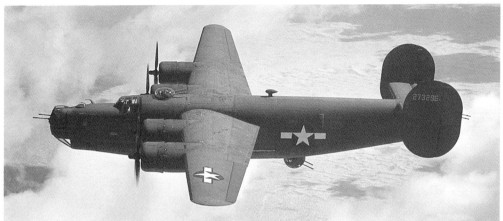

Left: The B-24 bomber, the aircraft involved in most of the foo-fighter incidents.

Below: This September 1946 U.S. government memo on ghost rockets was designated Top Secret.

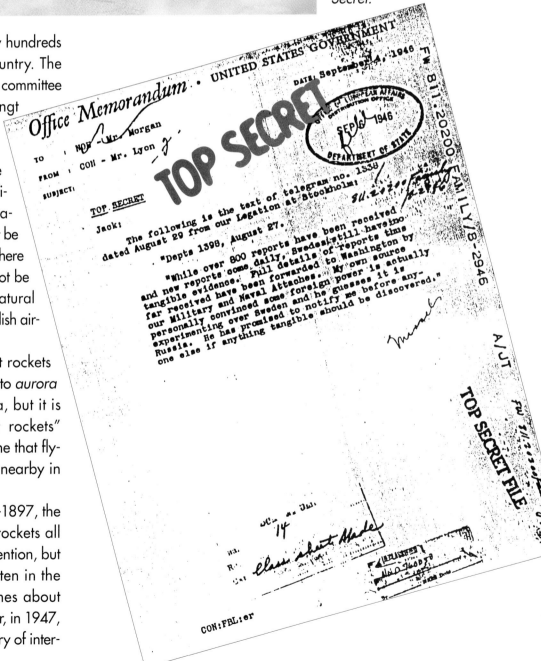

of light that had been seen by hundreds of people throughout the country. The Swedish government set up a committee under Air Commodore Bengt Jacobsson to evaluate ghost rockets and other flying objects, and on October 10, the Swedish Defense staff stated officially that most of the observations were vague and shouldn't be taken seriously, but added that there were some reports that "cannot be explained or written off as natural phenomena, and can't be Swedish aircraft or purely imagination."

Explanations for the ghost rockets ranged from meteor showers to *aurora borealis* to postwar hysteria, but it is interesting that the "ghost rockets" appeared about the same time that flying discs were first reported nearby in the Soviet Union.

The great airship of 1896–1897, the foo fighters, and the ghost rockets all generated a great deal of attention, but were soon gone and forgotten in the media, replaced by headlines about more tangible entities. However, in 1947, an incident would spark a flurry of interest that would not go away.

2: Kenneth Arnold Sights Flying Saucers

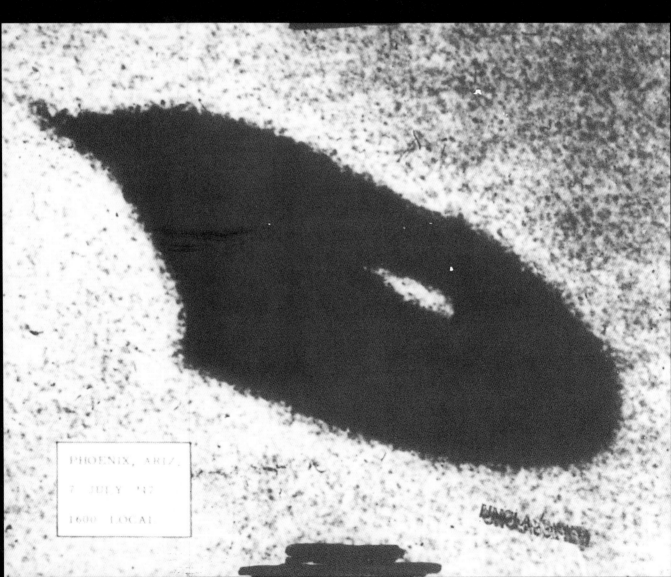

PHOENIX, ARIZ.

7 JULY '47

1600 LOCAL

UNCLASSIFIED

> ## "I've been convinced for a long time that the flying saucers are real and interplanetary. In other words, we are being watched by beings from outer space."
>
> —Albert M. Chop
> Deputy Public Relations Director, NASA;
> Former U.S. Air Force Spokesman, Project Blue Book

On the afternoon of Tuesday, June 24, 1947, a private pilot named Kenneth Arnold took off from the airport at Chehalis, Washington, en route to Yakima. The 32-year-old Boise, Idaho, businessman had no idea that he was about to fly into the opening scene of one of the largest controversies of the twentieth century.

The founder and chief salesman for Great Western Fire Control Supply, Arnold traveled the airways of the rural Northwest in his three-place Callair selling and installing firefighting equipment, and he had just completed a service call at Central Air Service in Chehalis. At about 2:00 PM, he took off. The air was smooth and visibility excellent, so Arnold decided to take time out to look for the wreckage of a Marine Corps R5C-1 Commando transport plane that had crashed some time before near Ashford, Washington, on the southwest slope of Mt. Rainier. Arnold approached the extinct volcano at 9,500 feet and then took the Callair lower to investigate some of the deep canyons on Rainier's south side. He turned at Mineral, Washington, and climbed back to 9,200 feet, noting a commercial Douglas DC-4 airliner behind and to his left, about 15 miles distant at 14,000 feet altitude.

Opposite: An object photographed on July 7, 1947, over Phoenix, Arizona.

Below: Kenneth Arnold: the man whose sighting gave rise to the term "flying saucers."

Above: *The majestic Mt. Rainier on a clear June afternoon. Arnold observed the formation of nine disc-shaped objects clearly against the snow-covered peak.*

Arnold's Saucers

Arnold trimmed out his airplane in the direction of Yakima, which was almost directly east of his position. The sky and air were entirely clear. At 2:59 PM, shortly after his turn, Arnold was startled by a bright flash that looked like the sun reflecting off a shiny object. Thinking he might be too close to another aircraft, Arnold quickly glanced around to locate the source of the reflection. He then observed a "chain" formation of nine aircraft to his left at roughly 9,500 feet and a heading of 170 degrees, rapidly approaching Mt. Rainier from the vicinity of Mt. Baker to the north. As these objects were quite far away, Arnold was unable for a few seconds to make out their shape or their formation. They soon approached Mt. Rainier, and he observed their outline against the snow quite plainly. He watched these objects with great interest, as he had never before observed airplanes flying so close to the mountaintops. Arnold assumed they were jet planes, although he thought it peculiar that he couldn't find their tails. He assumed that this was where the reflection had come from, as two or three of them every few seconds would dip or change their course slightly, just enough for the sun to strike them at an angle that reflected brightly on his plane.

They flew as he had observed geese flying, that is, in a diagonal line as if they were linked together. They seemed to hold a definite direction but swerved in and out of the high mountain peaks. The objects maintained an almost constant altitude. They did not seem to be going up or to be coming down, as would be the case with rockets or artillery shells. Arnold was convinced that they were some type of airplane. Their incredible speed did not impress him particularly, because he knew that the USAAF had airplanes that were very fast.

Arnold estimated his distance from them to be between 20 and 25 miles. He knew they must be very large for him to observe their shape at that distance. In fact, Arnold used a tool he had in his pocket to compare them, holding it up

on them and on the DC-4 that he had observed to his left. They seemed about a third smaller than the DC-4.

Arnold was particularly intrigued by the ability of the nine aircraft to maintain a close formation at high speed as they passed very near the mountain slopes. As they passed between him and the snow-covered peak, he observed from their silhouettes that they were disc-shaped aircraft without tails. By timing their flight between Mt. Rainier and Mt. Adams (about 40 miles distant), Arnold calculated their speed at 1,350 MPH.

Although Kenneth Arnold specifically mentioned that the military did not contact him during the summer of 1947, the case was analyzed for inclusion in the final report of Project Blue Book, the official U.S. Air Force review of UFOs. The Blue Book investigators noted that:

It is impossible to explain this incident away as sheer nonsense, if any credence at all is given to Mr. Arnold's integrity. However, certain

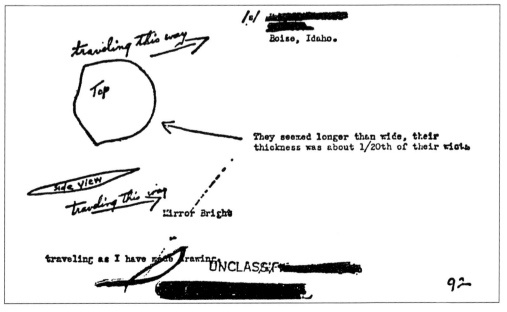

Left: Arnold's original sketch of the saucers, their location and flight path. His detailed notes and schematic diagrams of the size, shape and proportions are viewed as credible, given his experience and the conditions under which he observed the formation.

Who was Kenneth Arnold?

Kenneth Arnold, the man whose report touched off the flying saucer hysteria of 1947 and the unending interest in UFOs, was born March 29, 1915, in Subeka, Minnesota. He was a resident of Minnesota until he was six years old, when his family moved to Scobey, Montana, where they homesteaded. His grandfather also homesteaded in Scobey and became prominent in political circles as a colleague of Burton K. Wheeler, the famous Montana senator.

As a boy, Arnold was interested in athletics and was selected as an All-State end in 1932 and 1933 in North Dakota. He entered the United States Olympic diving trials in 1932. He was a Red Cross Life Saving Examiner and taught swimming and diving at scout camp and the municipal pool in Minot, North Dakota. He went to the University of Minnesota, where he swam under Neils Thorpe, and also played football under Bernie Bierman.

In 1938, Arnold went to work for Red Comet, Inc., of Littleton, Colorado, a manufacturer of automatic firefighting apparatus. In 1939 he was made district manager over a part of the Western states, and in 1940 he established his own company known as Great Western Fire Control Supply.

Arnold's flying experience started as a boy in Minot, North Dakota, where he took his first flying lesson. Due to the high cost, Arnold was unable to continue his flying, and he did not fly much until 1943, when he was given his pilot certificate by Ed Leach, a senior Civil Aeronautics Administration inspector at Portland, Oregon. From 1944, Arnold owned his own airplane, which he used in covering his entire sales territory, flying from 40 to 100 hours per month. In January 1947, he purchased a new Callair airplane, which was designed for high altitude takeoffs and short, rough field use. "In the type of flying I do," Arnold commented, "it takes a great deal of practice and judgment to be able to land in most any cow pasture and get out without injuring your airplane; the runways are very limited and the altitude is very high in some of the fields and places I have to go in my work."

Kenneth Arnold never asked for, nor wanted, any notoriety for accidentally being in the right spot at the right time to observe what he did. He reported something that he knew any pilot would have reported. When he landed at Yakima on June 24, 1947, and reported having seen "flying saucers," the news spread rapidly. Before the night was over, he was receiving telephone calls from all parts of the world. He said later that a number of USAAF pilots informed him that they had been briefed before going into combat overseas in World War II that they might see objects of similar shape and design to those he described, and they assured him that he wasn't dreaming or going crazy. Arnold quoted a former USAAF pilot who was then a crop duster at Pendleton, Oregon: "What you observed, I am convinced, is some type of jet or rocket-propelled ship that is in the process of being tested by our government, or even it could possibly be by some foreign government."

inconsistencies can be pointed out in the facts as reported: Arnold's attention was first drawn to the objects by a bright flash on his plane, which was followed by numerous other similar flashes. If these were something like the flash one gets from a distant mirror, it means that the reflection was specular, or direct. For a direct reflection, the angle between the observer, sun, and object must be "just right," and at such distances as 20 or 25 miles, the chance of a series of direct reflections is extremely small. If the object was a diffuse reflector—that is, scattering the sunlight falling on it, much as the moon or a balloon does—then at such a distance it seems quite unlikely that Mr. Arnold would have been startled, or that our attention would been called to it, unless the objects reflecting were extremely large.

The Air Force also called into question the supersonic speeds called for if Arnold's estimated distance was correct. "If Arnold's estimate of distance [20–25 miles] was correct, that of size [45–50 feet] cannot be, and vice versa." Blue Book felt it was logical to assume that his estimate of distance was far too great because that would have meant the objects had traveled 47 miles in 102 seconds—a rate of approximately 1,700 MPH—which was impossible with technology as it existed in the summer of 1947, when the world's absolute speed record stood officially at 624 MPH. However, it was not that far off, because the world's absolute speed record would

exceed 1,700 MPH in just nine years.

Blue Book concluded, based on their interpretation of Arnold's account, that the objects were 400 feet across and were traveling just 400 MPH. There was no mention of what aircraft then known was 400 feet across. The Boeing B-29, the largest aircraft then in use by the USAAF, had a wingspan of 141 feet. The Convair XB-36, with a wingspan of 230 feet, was the largest bomber ever built and only one such plane existed in June 1947.

Above: A model of a disc-shaped aircraft that was being developed secretly in the U.S. during the 1940s, demonstrated by Private Anderson in 1950. Arnold would have had no knowledge of such technology.

U.F.O. EVALUATING THE EVIDENCE

Below: *United Air Lines pilot Captain E.J. Smith and a stewardess describing to the press the nine "flying discs" they and their flight's copilot saw near Emmett, Idaho, on July 4, 1947. Their sighting, which coincided with 88 other reports of sightings (from a total of over 800 witnesses) on the same day, occurred just a few days before Johnson's at almost the same location (see page 38).*

The nine disc-shaped aircraft were visible for less than three minutes, but the die was cast for a controversy that would sweep the nation and the world for the next half century. Upon landing, Arnold described the flight pattern of the nine discs as being like that of "saucers" being "skipped across water." The news media seized upon his choice of words and the "flying saucer" term was born.

The Race For Tangible Evidence

After Arnold's observations became public, there was obvious interest by others to observe flying saucers. The media were driven to seek first publication of

photos of a "real" flying saucer. A half century later, the media are still waiting, but in the summer of 1947, it seemed that it might be a matter of days. One of the first to go looking for evidence was David Johnson, a private pilot with approximately 2,800 hours of flying time in equipment ranging from primary trainers to B-29 bombers.

On July 6, 1947, David Johnson was assigned by James L. Brown, general manager of Statesman Newspapers, to "conduct an aerial search of the northwest states in an effort to see and photograph a flying disc. Conduct this patrol for so long a time as you believe reasonable, or until you see a flying disc."

Left: The Maury Island affair (see next page) was investigated by USAAF personnel, who were only assigned the task after the Arnold sighting, although the "saucer" incident allegedly occurred on June 21. The investigators flew a B-25—to their deaths. Suspicions of foul play were never entirely dismissed.

In accordance with these instructions, Johnson took the Statesman's airplane, and, with Kenneth Arnold as a passenger, flew a nearly eight-hour mission on July 7, covering an area between Hanford, Washington, Mt. Rainier and Mt. Adams, where Arnold had first reported seeing flying saucers. They saw nothing that day, but on July 9, Johnson took off in an AT-6 trainer belonging to the 190th Fighter squadron of the Idaho National Guard (of which he was a member) on a flight which lasted approximately 2.5 hours. Johnson flew under and around rapidly forming cumulus clouds over that area known as the Camas Prairie, east of Boise. The clouds were near the town of Fairfield, 75 miles east of Boise.

At the time Johnson reached a point between Boise and Meridian, he was flying at an altitude of 14,000 feet mean sea level, which would be an average of 11,000 feet above ground. Johnson turned the aircraft and continued on an easterly heading, pointing toward Gowen Field, and had flown on that course for perhaps a minute when a round, black object appeared in the left portion of his field of view.

Johnson believed that he was seeing a weather balloon, and he called the Civil Aviation Administration communication station at Boise, and asked if the weather station had recently released a balloon. They had not done so since around 8:30 AM that day.

Upon hearing this response, Johnson turned the aircraft broadside to the object, pulled back the plexiglass covering to avoid any distortion, took his camera from the map case, and exposed about ten seconds' duration of 8mm motion picture film. During the time the camera (an f.1.9 Eastman) was at eye level, Johnson could not see the object because of the minuteness of the viewfinder's scope.

Taking the camera away and once again centering his gaze on the object,

Johnson observed it to roll so that its edge was presented to him. It flashed once in the sunlight, then appeared as a thin black line. It began a slow roll, or a barrel roll, to about the 180-degree point. The object rolled out of the top of the maneuver at this point, and Johnson lost sight of it. This entire sequence was observed against the backdrop of clouds over Camas Prairie. Johnson did not know how far away it was, nor could he estimate its speed.

Immediately after sighting the object, Johnson asked if there were other aircraft in the area. There was a P-51 of the 190th Fighter Squadron practicing maneuvers in the vicinity of Kuna, but that was behind him. A USAAF C-82 transport aircraft passed over Boise, but Johnson saw that aircraft go beneath him by some 2,000 feet. The P-51 in the vicinity of Kuna proceeded to the area where Johnson saw the object, at his request, and conducted a search. It was negative. During the afternoon, flights of P-51s were sent out to cover the area, and some of them flew high altitude missions on oxygen. These searches were negative.

Johnson was subsequently informed that personnel on both the United Air Lines side of Gowen Field, and on the Idaho National Guard side, had observed a black object maneuvering in front of the same cloud formation, which by now had grown so that the clouds reached an approximate altitude of 19,000–20,000 feet from a mean base of 13,000–14,000 feet mean sea level. Three of these men were National Guard personnel, and Johnson talked to them, asking them to describe what they saw,

before telling them his story, in order to avoid suggestion or inference of a leading nature. They saw the object (from the ground) while Johnson was on his second search. They reported that the object performed in the same erratic manner that Johnson had observed.

The question remains, of course, whether Johnson saw it and whether or not it could have been a weather balloon. The movie film, developed and processed by R.W. Stohr in the Eastman laboratories in San Francisco, showed no trace of any object. Stohr reported that if it was more than a mile distant from the camera at the size Johnson described, the object would not have registered sufficiently on the small-format 8mm film to be shown. He said it probably was too far away, and Johnson did not have a telephoto lens on his camera.

The Maury Island Mystery

U.S. Army Air Forces interest in the UFO phenomena had actually been sparked by an event which preceded the Kenneth Arnold sighting by three days and the Roswell Incident (next chapter) by a week and a half.

On June 21, 1947, over Maury Island in Puget Sound near Tacoma, Washington, less than 100 air miles from Mt. Rainier, two harbor patrolmen reported seeing a "flying saucer" explode. Though the incident allegedly occurred on June 21, the USAAF was actually contacted *after* the Arnold incident.

The incident is notable both for being the first elaborate hoax of the flying saucer era and for being the first instance of USAAF personnel being killed in line with an investigation of the phenomena. Captain William Davidson and Lieutenant Frank M. Brown were dispatched from Hamilton Army Air Field north of San Francisco, the headquarters of both the Fourth Air Force and the Western Air Defense Force, an element of the USAAF (termed U.S. Air Force after September 18, 1947) Air Defense Command, to investigate the matter.

Davidson and Brown flew in a B-25 to McChord Army Air Field and drove to nearby Tacoma, where they met the two harbor patrolmen and a third party in a hotel room. They were shown some fragments of metal slag that was supposedly the remnants of the exploded "inner-tube-shaped" aircraft. One version of the story has it that the two officers took the material with them, while the official version states that they rejected the incident as a hoax and left the slag behind. The two officers themselves were not able to shed any light on the event because they were killed early on August 1, 1947, when their B-25 crashed near Kelso, Washington, shortly after they took off on their flight home. Because they died "mysteriously" while in the midst of a flying saucer evaluation, the deaths of Captain Davidson and Lieutenant Brown provided a good deal of grist for conspiracy theorists, but the perpetrators later admitted that the incident had been a publicity stunt.

With two airmen dead in the midst of a flurry of flying saucer reports that began with Arnold, the USAAF was compelled by public opinion to take the phenomena seriously. It is certain that *if* the disc-

shaped aircraft were being operated as a highly secret USAAF program, most of that service knew *nothing* about it and reacted with the same concern about the reports as did the general public.

The Maury Island investigation had been undertaken by the Fourth Air Force because it happened to be within the Fourth's geographical region. Other "local" commands undertook similar evaluations in the absence of any centralized directive on the matter. Within a matter of weeks, however, the USAAF would become officially involved in evaluating flying saucers, but events were moving more quickly than anyone realized.

Above: *Harry S. Truman had acquired specialized knowledge of the aviation industry before he assumed the presidency in April 1945, having investigated military spending as head of a senatorial committee founded at his own instigation.*

3: The Roswell Incident and a Host of Sightings

Leased Wire
Associated Press

Roswell Daily Record

RECORD PHONES
Business Office 2288
News Department 2287

VOL 46. NUMBER 99 ESTABLISHED 1888   ROSWELL, NEW MEXICO, TUESDAY, JULY 8, 1947   5c PER COPY.

Movies as Usual

Levees broke and flood waters rolled into the town of Grand Tower, Ill., but while the manager of this movie theater sweeps out the water that has entered the lobby, these youngsters are standing in line for tickets for the night's performance. (AP Wirephoto)

Some of Soviet Satellites May Attend Paris Meeting

Paris, July 8 (AP) — Indications mounted today that at least some of the nations within the Soviet orbit would attend the Paris conference in the Marshall aid-to-talks.

A Sofia dispatch quoted an authoritative source as saying probably Bulgaria will participate in the conference, which opens in Paris Saturday. The dispatch said the Bulgarian council of ministers was meeting to reach a decision in the matter.

Despite a Moscow radio report that Yugoslavia had rejected the British-French invitation to participate, observers in Belgrade said the Yugoslavs still had not replied, and probably will not do so before Thursday—the deadline for an answer. Dr. Ales Debler,

Roswellians Have Differing Opinions On Flying Saucers

Roswell is a bit uncertain about those flying disks it would appear from interviews today with a number of local citizens with about as many ideas concern-

Claims Army Is Stacking Courts Martial

Indiana Senator Lays Protest Before Patterson

Washington, July 8 (AP)—Senator Jenner (R-Ind.) contended today that "the high command in the European theatre is stacking courts against defendants in court martial."

In a letter to Secretary of War Patterson demanding a full investigation of army military trial procedure, Jenner offered what he said was documentary proof that:

1. "Prisoners are not being permitted to employ either civilian or military counsel of their own choice in the preparation and presentation of their defense."

2. "Every effort is being made to prevent attorneys who were connected with the infamous Lichfield prison case to practice in courts martial in the European theatre."

The Indiana senator made public a copy of an informal "routing slip" which he said was signed by Brig. Gen. Cornelius E. Ryan, assistant deputy, military government headquarters for the military government for Germany, and written by Col. Francis H. Vanderwerker. Jenner told newsmen that the routing slip substantiated his charges.

The slip, addressed to the chief of staff, USFET (presumably US forces, European theatre), was dated last Oct. 21.

It called attention to the impending arrival of Earl J. Carroll and Thomas Lester Poley, California attorneys, to act as special defense counsel for five prisoners then awaiting trial by general court martial at Frankfurt AM Main.

Jenner identified Carroll as counsel in the court martial of Col James A. Kilian in the Lichfield (England) prison brutality case.

Carroll, then an army captain, resigned as assistant prosecutor in the Lichfield trials after asserting that a deliberate attempt was being made by army legal authorities to whitewash higher officers in the case. Kilian was later convicted and fined.

The routing slip said that Carroll had received widespread publicity "by violent attacks on the system of military justice" and added "it is understood that Poley is an individual of similar pro-

House Passes Tax Slash by Large Margin

Defeat Amendment By Demos to Remove Many from Rolls

Washington, July 8 (AP)—The house passed today the Republican-backed bill to cut income taxes by $4,000,000,000 annually for 40,000,000 taxpayers, beginning Jan. 1.

It goes to the senate where approval also is forecast.

The vote was 302 to 11, or more than the two-thirds majority needed to override a presidential veto.

The action, which may encounter another presidential veto, came after Speaker Martin (R-Mass.) personally appealed to the house to pass the bill by such a decisive vote—as to persuade the president that the people should have this delayed justice."

The measure is identical with one vetoed by President Truman June 16 as "the wrong kind of tax reduction at the wrong time" —except that the effective date is changed from July 1, 1947 to Jan. 1, 1948.

Congress leaders expect to have the revised bill on Mr. Truman's desk before the week ends.

The house passed the bill after the Republicans beat back a proposed Democratic substitute that would have reduced taxes by $3,-279,000,000 and removed 4,000,000 low-income persons from the tax rolls completely.

American League Wins All-Star Game

Chicago, July 8 (AP) — The American league, pecking away with an eight-hit attack and ringing the bell with its pinch-

Security Council Paves Way to Talks On Arms Reductions

Lake Success, July 8 (AP)—The United Nations security council today approved an American blueprint for arms reduction discussions despite a Russian warning that the plan would bring about a collapse of arms regulation efforts.

The vote was 9 to 0 with Russia and Poland abstaining.

In view of Russia's firm stand against the U. S. plan it had been believed she might invoke the big power veto to block it.

Soviet Deputy Foreign Minister Andrei A. Gromyko gave his warning before the United Nations security council in a new effort to revive the Soviet working plan which already had been rejected by the commission for conventional armaments.

His challenge was taken up promptly by French delegate Alexandre Parodi and U. S. Representative Herschel V. Johnson, who announced their opposition to any substitute for the American plan.

Gromyko insisted that no program for arms regulation could succeed unless the plan linked directly with absolute prohibition of atomic weapons.

He declared that the U.S. plan approved by the commission did not link the problems of arms regulation and the banning of atomic weapons and, for this reason, it offered no basis for a solution.

Gromyko opened debate on the arms question as delegates awaited another major declaration from him later in the day in reply to United States and British demands for action to restore order in the critical Balkan situation.

Delegates agreed they were approaching perhaps the gravest moment in U. N. history.

RAAF Captures Flying Saucer On Ranch in Roswell Region

No Details of Flying Disk Are Revealed

Roswell Hardware Man and Wife Report Disk Seen

The intelligence office of the 509th Bombardment group at Roswell Army Air Field announced at noon today, that the field had come into possession of a flying saucer.

According to information released by the department, over authority of Maj. J. A. Marcel, intelligence officer, the disk was recovered on a ranch in the Roswell vicinity, after an unidentified rancher had notified Sheriff Geo. Wilcox, here, that he had found the instrument on his premises.

Major Marcel and a detail from his department went to the ranch and recovered the disk, it was stated.

After the intelligence office here had inspected the instrument it was flown to "higher headquarters."

The intelligence office stated that no details of the saucer's construction or its appearance had been revealed.

Mr. and Mrs. Dan Wilmot apparently were the only persons in Roswell who have seen what they thought was a flying disk.

They were sitting on their porch at 105 South Penn. last Wednesday night at about ten minutes before ten o'clock when a large glowing object zoomed out of the sky from the southeast, going in a northwesterly direction at a high rate of speed.

Wilmot called Mrs. Wilmot's attention to it and both ran down into the yard to watch. It was in sight less than a minute, perhaps 40 or 50 seconds. Wilmot estimated.

Wilmot said that it appeared to him to be about 1,500 feet high and going fast. He estimated between 400 and 500 miles per hour.

Ex-King Carol Weds Mme. Lupescu

Former King Carol of Romania and Mme. Elena Lupescu relax aboard the S. S. America bound for Cuba and Mexico in May, 1941. A member of Carol's household in Rio de Janeiro said the ex-king and his companion for 23 years in reign and exile were recently married at their hotel Copacabana Palace suite. (AP Wirephoto)

Miners and Operators Sign Highest Wage Pact in History

Washington, July 8 (AP)—An agreement averting a nation-wide soft coal strike was signed today by John L. Lewis and a majority of the bituminous operators.

In announcing the signing, Lewis told a news conference that it is "reasonable to assume" the entire industry will accept the agreement within a few

An official of the UMW told reporters union district presidents immediately started notifying miners to report for work at pits owned by the operators who signed the agreement.

There have been on a 10-day vacation, which ended last night. Lewis had told them to await the formal signing of the contract be-

> **"The Bureau...has agreed to cooperate in the investigation of flying discs....Air Force Intelligence has also indicated some concern that the reported sightings might have been made by subversive individuals for the purpose of creating a mass hysteria."**
>
> —FBI, Authorization to Investigate, July 30, 1947

On July 4, 1947, a week after Arnold's sighting, one of the most important events in the annals of UFO lore occurred near Roswell, New Mexico. It was to be the first case of a UFO reportedly recovered by military personnel. Though the Roswell Incident was widely reported at the time, it was soon officially dismissed by the USAAF and promptly dropped by the media. The event received little coverage until the 1980s, when reports about recovery of the craft's occupants began to circulate. It is not clear why the Roswell event was overlooked for so long by both official and unofficial UFO investigators, but it should be remembered that in the late 1940s, a government denial was far more believable than it would be in the post-Vietnam/post-Watergate environment a generation later.

The Roswell Incident was actually a series of events that included a number of both radar and visual sightings of fast-moving silvery discs by credible observers between June 29 and July 4 over the U.S. Army's White Sands Missile Range, about 75 miles west of Roswell. On the evening of July 2, retailer Dan Wilmot and his wife saw such an object over Roswell itself.

A Crash in the Desert

On Independence Day, July 4, a thunderstorm rolled into eastern New Mexico, as such storms often do during that time of year. White Sands radar was tracking a fast-moving object over the town of Corona, 75 miles northwest of Roswell, when it disappeared from the scope. At the same time, several people near Corona heard an explosion in the nearby desert. The following morning, a group of archaeology students and two vacationers arrived to observe the crash site of what was reportedly a wedge-shaped aircraft. The USAAF also arrived on the scene that morning, but apparently did

Opposite: The July 8, 1947, issue of the Roswell Daily Record, reporting the incident that would cause a sensation worldwide.

not secure the area for at least 24 hours. Major Jesse Marcel, the Intelligence Officer of the 509th Bomb Group, stationed at Roswell Army Air Field (RAAF), visited the scene and issued an official statement saying that a flying saucer had been found. Nothing was said about the discovery of bodies aboard it, although several witnesses would claim 40 years later that they had seen small corpses with smooth yellow skin either at the site or in USAAF custody.

Despite the charges of cover-up and countercharges of sensationalism, there is no disputing that something happened in the Roswell area in July 1947. It was reported in a number of contemporary newspapers, notably the July 8 and 9 editions of the *Roswell Daily Record*. The July 8 edition reported, "RAAF Captures Flying Saucer On Ranch In Roswell Region," while the next day's *Record* reported that Eighth Air Force commander General Roger Ramey had "emptied" the Roswell Saucer. Another, somewhat ominous, headline read: "Harassed Rancher Who Located 'Saucer' Sorry He Told About It."

The first story reported that Major Marcel had recovered a flying disc from the range lands of an unidentified rancher in the vicinity of Roswell and that the disc had been "flown to higher headquarters." It was also reported that a Roswell couple claimed to have seen a large object fly by their home on July 2, 1947.

Below: *Seasonal thunderclouds forming over Roswell. Such storms can build to an alarming and destructive intensity—sufficient to cause an air disaster.*

The "harassed rancher" was W.W. Brazel of Lincoln County, New Mexico. He claimed that he and his son, Vernon, "came upon a large area of bright wreckage made up of rubber strips, metallic foil, a rather tough paper, and sticks." He picked up some of the debris on July 4. Next day he heard about the flying discs and wondered if his find might have been the remnants of one of these craft. Brazel went to Roswell on July 7 and contacted the sheriff, who apparently notified Major Marcel. The major and "a man in plain clothes" then accompanied Brazel home to pick up the rest of the pieces. The newspaper article further related that Brazel believed the material:

might have been as large as a tabletop. The balloon which held it up, if that is how it worked, must have been about 12 feet long, he felt, measuring the distance by the size of the room in which he sat. The rubber was smoky gray in color and scattered over an area about 200 yards in diameter. When the debris was gathered up, the metallic foil, paper, tape, and sticks made a bundle about three feet long and seven or eight inches thick, while the rubber made a bundle about 18 or 20 inches long and about eight inches thick. In all, he estimated, the entire lot would have weighed maybe five pounds.

Above: General Hoyt Vandenburg, Deputy Chief of Staff of the U.S. Air Force, was believed to have been involved in the investigation of the Roswell incident.

U.F.O. EVALUATING THE EVIDENCE

There was no sign in the area of any metal that might have been used for an engine, and no sign of any propellers of any kind. At least one paper fin had been glued onto some of the metallic foil, but there were no words to be found anywhere on the instrument, although there were letters on some of the parts. Considerable Scotch tape and some tape with flowers printed upon it had been used in the construction. No string or wire were found, but there were some eyelets in the paper to indicate that some sort of attachment may have been used.

Brazel also said that he had previously found two weather balloons on the ranch, but that this debris did not resemble either of the balloons.

A Troubled Summer

The summer of 1947 saw a media frenzy that galvanized public preoccupation with the flying saucer phenomenon. Within two weeks of the Arnold report, an epidemic of sightings occurred throughout the American Far West.

On July 4, just as something was falling out of the sky near Corona, New Mexico, several people (including police officers) observed disc-shaped objects over Portland, Oregon, roughly 100 air miles from Mt. Rainier. At Twin Falls, Idaho, a crowd of 60 people at an Independence Day picnic saw discs "flying in V-formation, while others circled and divided in loose formation." Not far away, at Hauser Lake, some 200 people watching a baseball game observed a disc-shaped object above them for 30 minutes, before it zoomed vertically out of sight. The wave of July 4 sightings continued when, at 9:12 PM, Captain E.J. Smith and his copilot, Ralph Stevens, who were flying a United Airlines DC-3 out of Boise, Idaho (Arnold's hometown), observed nine discs flying in two formations over Emmett, Idaho, at an altitude of 7,100 feet.

Four days later, on July 8, military personnel at the USAAF's secret flight test center at Muroc Army Air Field (now Edwards AFB) in California reported overflights by unusual objects. At 9:30 AM, several witnesses saw three silvery spheres traveling at about 300 MPH against the wind. A yellowish-white sphere was seen by a test pilot 40 minutes later, traveling at 200 MPH against the wind. Two hours later, a crew of technicians at nearby Rogers Dry Lake saw another object that was "white aluminum color, which at first resembled a parachute canopy. As the object fell, it drifted slightly north of due west against the prevailing wind....No smoke, flames, propeller arcs, engine noise, or other plausible or visible means of propulsion were noted. The color was silver, resembling an aluminum-painted fabric, and did not appear as dense as a parachute canopy....It is estimated that the object was in sight about 90 seconds."

At about 4:00 PM that afternoon, the pilot of an F-51 flying at 20,000 feet saw "a flat object of a light-reflecting nature" lacking "a vertical fin or wings." The pilot estimated its postion as about 40 miles south of Muroc.

The commander of the 509th Bomb Group at Roswell Army Air Field, Colonel William H. "Butch" Blanchard, went on leave on July 8, 1947. This would have been somewhat unusual for a person involved in the supposed first-ever recovery of extraterrestrial materials. However, it has been suggested that Blanchard "took leave" as a ploy to elude the press and went to the scene to direct recovery operations.

It is also suggested that something unusual might have been going on when Lieutenant General Nathan Twining (illustrated above), commander of the Air Matériel Command, traveled to New Mexico in July 1947. In the 1994 investigation, the Air Force would locate records "indicating that Twining went to the Bomb Commanders' Course on July 8, along with a number of other general officers, and requested orders to do so a month before, on June 5, 1947."

Meanwhile, General Hoyt Vandenberg, Deputy Chief of Staff (and soon after, Chief of Staff), was also alleged to be involved in investigations at Roswell. Later, activity reports located in General Vandenberg's personal papers stored in the Library of Congress did indicate that on July 7 he was busy with a "flying disc" incident. However, this incident involved Ellington Field, Texas, and the Spokane, Washington, Depot. After much discussion and information-gathering on the Roswell incident, the Air Force determined it to be a hoax.

Cover-up in Fort Worth?

The July 9 edition of the *Roswell Daily Record* noted that Brigadier General Roger Ramey, Commander of the Eighth Air Force at Forth Worth, Texas, stated that, upon examination, the debris recovered by Major Jesse Marcel was determined to be a weather balloon. The wreckage was described as a "bundle of metallic foil, broken wood beams, and rubber remnants of a balloon...."

Major Marcel would later claim that the pieces of debris he brought from the crash site were replaced by pieces of a weather balloon just before he met with reporters at Fort Worth. The following day, the USAAF officially announced that the alleged "flying saucer" was really a weather balloon. The news media accepted this as the last word, and public interest in the story evaporated.

During the 1980s, journalists began to rediscover an event that had gone virtually unnoticed for over four decades. Writers Charles Berlitz and William Moore spoke with numerous people who claimed to have had firsthand experience with the crashed aircraft and its inhabitants: they reported that military authorities had coerced them into keeping quiet. Thanks to Berlitz's and Moore's 1980 book *Incident At Roswell,* and subsequent books by Kevin Randle and Donald Schmitt, the events of July 4, 1947, became the definitive UFO cover-up story of the 1990s. A 1994 TV movie called *Roswell* was based on their book *The Truth About the UFO Crash at Roswell*. The following year, an alleged documentary of the autopsy of one of the "aliens" recovered from the UFO was aired on television. Kal K. Korff's book *The Roswell UFO Crash: What They Don't Want You to Know* (1997) examines critically the recent claims of these researchers and new witnesses.

U.F.O. EVALUATING THE EVIDENCE

Below: As well as assessing reports of sightings, investigators relied on specialists to examine physical evidence, including photographs, radar records and debris. The alleged wreckage of a flying saucer shown below was determined to be a hoax produced with commonly available parts—one of many time-consuming fakes exposed at the height of UFO reporting.

The Air Force Gets Involved

Despite having been drawn into the "flying saucer" mystery from Maury Island to Muroc to Roswell, the USAAF was apparently slow to develop a coherent policy on the phenomenon. It may well be that official reaction was tempered by the massive reorganization of the American military establishment in the summer of 1947. On July 26, President Harry Truman had signed the National Security Act of 1947, which abolished the old War and Navy Departments and established a single Department of Defense that would oversee the Army and Navy. It also transformed the U.S. Army Air Forces into the completely independent U.S. Air Force, on equal footing with the Army and Navy.

It was not until September 18, however, that the U.S. Air Force was officially "born" out of the wartime USAAF, and General Carl "Tooey" Spaatz, Chief of Staff of the USAAF, was not officially sworn in as U.S. Air Force Chief of Staff until September 26. During these critical days in the evolution of the flying saucer phenomenon, the USAAF/U.S. Air Force was in a state of transition. However, five days after the USAAF became the independent U.S. Air Force, the new service was officially in the business of flying saucer evaluation.

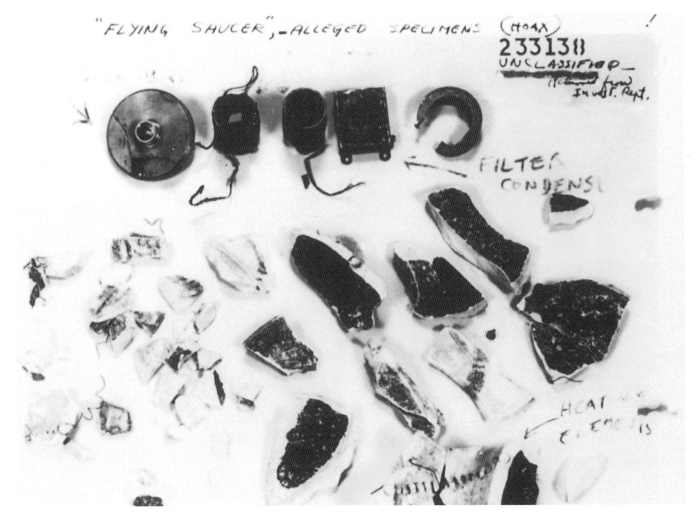

Actually, the USAAF had been looking into flying saucer reports since the Maury Island affair, but these efforts were undertaken at lower levels and not under central command. In the first few months, the USAAF had begun to evaluate UFO reports that came to its attention at the Air Technical Intelligence Center (ATIC), part of the Air Matériel Command (AMC), located at Wright-Patterson AFB near Dayton, Ohio.

It was on September 23, 1947, that the AMC commander, Lieutenant General Nathan Farragut Twining, wrote to his boss, General Spaatz, about "flying saucers." Twining told Spaatz that he was concerned about the "so-called flying discs" and wanted to see them officially evaluated. He advised Spaatz and Brigadier General George Schulgen of the Air Force Office of Research and Development that he had reviewed the reports and had discussed the subject with personnel of the AMC Engineering Division and the Air Institute of Technology. It was their opinion that the "phenomenon is something real and not visionary or fictitious."

General Twining went on to describe the reports and to speculate that there was a "possibility that these objects are of domestic origin—the product of some high security project not known to AC/AS-2 [the Headquarters Air Staff] or the Command [AMC]." He also conceded "the possibility that some foreign nation has a form of propulsion, possibly nuclear, which is outside our domestic knowledge." He recommended that the U.S. Air Force: "Issue a directive assigning a priority, security classifica-

tion and Code Name for a detailed evaluation of this matter, to include the preparation of complete sets of all available and pertinent data which will then be made available to the Army, Navy, Atomic Energy Commission, the Air Force Scientific Advisory Group, the National Advisory Committee for Aeronautics (NACA), and the Rand and other projects for comments and recommendations."

In the meantime, Twining directed the AMC to "confine the investigation within its current resources in order to more closely define the nature of the phenomena." What he had in mind was a serious, full-scale effort to get to the bot-

Above: General Carl "Tooey" Spaatz was commander of all USAAF strategic forces in Europe during World War II, and became chief of staff of the U.S. Air Force in September 1947. The first Air Force UFO investigations were conducted under his command.

tom of the whole business in a matter of months. What came about instead was a 22-year, low-level effort that yielded an inconclusive report based on analyses of largely extraneous material. Many have speculated that there was also a parallel evaluation apparatus that was much better funded, much more thorough, and kept top secret.

At Wright-Patterson, Twining convened an impressive panel of expert investigators and evidence evaluators, including personnel from the Air Institute of Technology, the Intelligence Office, the Chief of Engineering Division, and the Aircraft, Power Plant and Propeller Laboratories of the Engineering Division. They decided that the phenomena reported were real and that they were objects approximating the shape of a disc, and apparently as large as man-made aircraft. They also discussed the possibility that some of the incidents might have been caused by such natural phenomena as meteors.

The Air Matériel Command panel looked into the reported operating characteristics, including extreme rates of climb, maneuverability (particularly in roll), and action that appeared evasive when sighted by friendly aircraft and radar. They believed that this lent credence to the possibility that some of the objects were controlled, either manually or remotely.

Air Matériel Command concluded, in part, that it knew of no such aircraft, but that it was possible—within the limits of 1947 technology—to construct a quiet, piloted aircraft that was circular or elliptical in shape, flat on the bottom and domed on top, with a metallic reflecting surface. With a possible nod to the vehicle purportedly recovered near Roswell, New Mexico, Twining noted that "crash-recovered exhibits...would undeniably prove the existence of these objects."

Project Sign

General Twining's official reply from Washington finally came on December 30, more than three months after his original memo recommending an investigation. It was signed by Chief of Staff Major General L.C. Craigie, director of Research & Development in the office of the Deputy Chief of Staff for Matériel. This memo stated that: "It is Air Force policy not to ignore reports of sightings and phenomena in the atmosphere, but to recognize that part of its mission is to collect, collate, evaluate and act on information of this nature."

Craigie's outline described, in essence, what AMC's Air Technical Intelligence Center (ATIC) was already doing. Now, however, the project had been given a "restricted" security classification and had been officially named "Project Sign." By the time this memo reached General Twining's desk at Wright-Patterson AFB, the media firestorm had given the flying saucer sensation a life of its own. Newspapers nationwide, including *The New York Times,* were running articles almost daily, and the rash of sightings was featured in such major magazines as *Life, Look, Newsweek* and *Time.* There was speculation that the UFOs were either secret American or secret Soviet aircraft, but the Air Force officially denied both possibilities.

During the period between June and December 1947, partly because of the disruption arising from the USAAF-to-U.S. Air Force transition, there was no specific organization responsible for investigating and evaluating the UFO evidence. But the wide news coverage of public UFO reports created sufficient concern at high military levels to prompt the Air Matériel Command to authorize and conduct a preliminary evaluation of these reports.

Begun in January 1948 and concluded in February 1949, Project Sign would evaluate 243 UFO reports submitted to it. The report concluded that "No definite and conclusive evidence is yet available that would prove or disprove the existence of these UFOs as real aircraft of unknown and unconventional configuration." When it began, the project was classified Top Secret. In his December 1952 Air Force briefing on UFOs for the Air Defense Command, Captain Edward Ruppelt remarked that: "This is probably the reason for the rumors that the Air Force has Top Secret information on this subject; it does not. The only reason for the original classification was that when the project first started the people on the project did not know what they were dealing with and, therefore, unknowingly put on this high classification."

The XF5U-1

In the midst of speculation about the flying discs, it was suggested that they might be a development of the Vought

Below: The U.S. Navy's Vought XF5U-1, appropriately nicknamed the "Flying Pancake," a disc-shaped aircraft that was scrapped just two years after the first (and only) example was completed.

XF5U-1, an experimental circular-flying wing fighter aircraft that had been designed by Charles H. Zimmerman and developed for the U.S. Navy during World War II. The design had been test flown in an unmanned wooden mock-up form as Vought model V-173 on November 23, 1942. On July 15, 1944, the Navy ordered two prototypes under the XF5U-1 designation (USN Bureau of Aeronautics serial numbers 33958 and 33959). Officially named "Skimmer" or "Zimmer Skimmer" (and unofficially called the "Flying Pancake" or "Flying Flapjack"), the XF5U-1 was nearly circular (28 ft. 1½ in. long and 23 ft. 4 in. across). It was to have been powered by two Pratt & Whitney R-2000-2, 1,600 HP turbo supercharged radial engines that drove two huge four-bladed pro-

pellers designed to lift the fighter off a small space on an aircraft carrier's deck, like a helicopter.

The first XF5U-1 was finished in August 1945 (with 1350 HP R-2000-7 engines used because the intended power plant wasn't ready yet). By this time, the war was almost over and the Navy chose to cancel the second prototype and not to flight-test the first because

it would have required expensive surface shipment from the Vought plant to Muroc Field, California. In March of that pivotal year—1947—the lone XF5U-1 was cut up for scrap without ever having gone into production.

One line of speculation in the wake of the saucer sightings of 1947 was that an advanced "Flying Pancake" had actually been secretly developed and was the source of the sightings. However, the XF5U-1 would have had a top speed of just 479 MPH, even with the specified engines. This was a respectable speed for a World War II fighter, but far from the supersonic 1,350 MPH of the discs that Kenneth Arnold had observed. Indeed, no piston-engined aircraft would have been capable of supersonic speeds—and certainly not in level flight. Thus, no evolution of the XF5U-1 design could account for the performance being reported in the flying disc observations.

Over the coming years and decades, any number of aircraft would be linked to the flying saucer mystery. Perhaps the best known is the VZ-9-AV Avrocar that was built by Avro of Canada in 1958. Curiously, it was built under contract for both the U.S. Army and the U.S. Air Force. Perfectly disc-shaped, with a diameter of 18 feet, twin cockpits and three vectored-thrust engines, it was the only round aircraft whose existence was officially acknowledged. Reports are that it had stability problems and never flew more than a few feet off the ground. The single prototype (serial number 58-7055) is preserved at the U.S. Army Transportation Museum at Fort Eustis, Virginia.

Left: French "flying saucer" technology: a 25-foot-wide aircraft, with its designer, René Couzinet, who claimed it was capable of speeds up to 1,000 MPH. The aircraft was first displayed to the public in 1955 in this hangar in Brighton, England.

"Of course the flying saucers are real and they are interplanetary."

—Air Chief Marshal Lord Dowding
Commanding officer, Royal Air Force, August 1954

By the beginning of 1948, the media may well have been ready to take an interest in something other than flying saucers. But a new development would soon rivet the public's attention to the phenomena: the saucers were about to "claim" their first victim. On the afternoon of January 7, less than a week after General Nathan Twining received the memo from Air Force headquarters directing him to undertake Project Sign, a sudden flurry of flying disc sightings was reported over Maysville, on the Ohio-Kentucky state line, only 75 air miles south of Twining's office at Wright-Patterson AFB. In this case, the observers included not only pilots, but Air Force control tower personnel, who watched the UFO for more than half an hour.

Thomas Mantell's Fatal Close Encounter

At approximately 2:00 PM, Kentucky State Police reported to Fort Knox Military Police that they had sighted an unusual aircraft or object flying through the air. It was circular in appearance, approximately 250–300 feet in diameter, and moving westward at "a pretty good clip." This, in turn, was reported to the commanding officer at Godman Field, Fort Knox, who called Godman Tower and asked Flight Service to check with Flight Test at Wright Field to see if they had any experimental aircraft in the area.

A Captain Hooper at Flight Test Operations stated, "We have no experimental aircraft in that area. However, we do have a B-29 and an A-26 on photo missions." Godman Tower reported that there was a large light in the sky in the approximate position of the object seen earlier. Then Lockbourne Tower and Clinton County Tower reported that a great ball of light was traveling southwest across the sky.

Between 2:30 and 2:40 PM, a loose formation of four Air National Guard F-51 Mustang fighter aircraft, en route from Marietta, Georgia, to Standiford Field (at Louisville, Kentucky), passed near Godman Field. Sergeant Quinton Blackwell, a tower operator who had been the first observer to see the mystery object over Godman, asked the Air Guard flight leader to attempt to identify it. Colonel Guy Hix, Blackwell's commanding officer, underscored the request. Three of the four turned south to a heading of 210 degrees to intercept the unknown object, while the fourth, being

Opposite: The tail of Captain Thomas F. Mantell's crashed P-51 Mustang, found near Franklin, Kentucky, on January 7, 1948. Mantell was last heard from as he was "trying to close in for a better look" at the UFO he was attempting to intercept.

Above: *North American Aviation's P-51 Mustang is considered among the most reliable fighter aircraft of its time.*

short of fuel, continued on to Standiford Field. At 2:45 PM Captain Thomas F. Mantell, Jr., the flight leader, reported that he had sighted the object "ahead and above." The other pilots turned back because they were not completely outfitted for flights to altitudes requiring oxygen. They attempted to contact Captain Mantell by radio but were unsuccessful.

It should be pointed out here that the North American Aviation F-51 Mustang (P-51 prior to 1947) was in its element intercepting an unidentified aircraft under these circumstances. Developed during World War II by North American Aviation, the P-51 saw worldwide service with the USAAF and Allied air forces, and is generally considered one of the best air superiority fighters of the war. Many people consider the definitive variant, the P-51D, to have been the best piston-engined fighter in history. Thirty months after the war ended, the first-line Air Force units had been equipped with jet fighters, but the Mustang, now in service with the Air

National Guard, was no less a scrapper than it had been over Germany or Japan in 1945.

Mantell ascended to 15,000 feet, whereupon he radioed, "Object directly ahead and above and moving about half my speed." Moments later he reported, "It appears metallic and of tremendous size." Still later, "I'm still climbing....Object is above and ahead, moving about my speed or faster....I'm trying to close in for a better look."

Captain Mantell's transmission at 15,000 feet was the last that was heard from him. The fragmented wreckage of his F-51 was found on a farm near Franklin, Kentucky. Mantell's body was in the cockpit, and there was no evidence that he had tried to bail out. This led some people to speculate that the F-51 had been "fired upon" by the UFO. Some newspaper accounts mentioned that traces of radioactivity were found at the site. This led to further headlines suggesting that an "atomic ray" had shot Mantell down.

Maxwell Flight Service Center called Franklin, Kentucky, and spoke to police officer Joe Walker, who took charge at the scene of the accident. Officer Walker stated that when he arrived, the pilot's body had been removed from the aircraft. Upon questioning eyewitnesses, Officer Walker learned that the aircraft had exploded in the air but had not burned when it hit the ground. The wreckage was scattered over an area of about one mile; the tail section and one wing had not yet been found.

In investigating the incident, the Air Technical Intelligence Center (ATIC)

decided that Captain Mantell had lost consciousness due to oxygen starvation, since the plane continued to climb until the altitude caused a sufficient loss of power to cause the F-51 to level out. The aircraft then began a turn to the left: as the wing drooped, so did the nose, until the plane went into a diving spiral. The rapid, uncontrolled descent caused it to disintegrate. The belief that Mantell had never regained consciousness was borne out by the fact that the canopy lock was still in place after the crash.

There were two official explanations of the UFO's identity. According to the first theory, the object could have been the planet Venus, one of the brightest objects in the sky. At the time of the sighting, Venus was in a position which coincided with that of the UFO. The planet's angular distance from the sun was rather small, but it was still bright enough to be seen by day. It is possible that Venus was the cause of this sighting and was observed by some of the witnesses on the ground.

Below: *The forward fuselage of Mantell's crashed P-51. The debris was scattered over a wide area, indicating that the plane had disintegrated during its descent.*

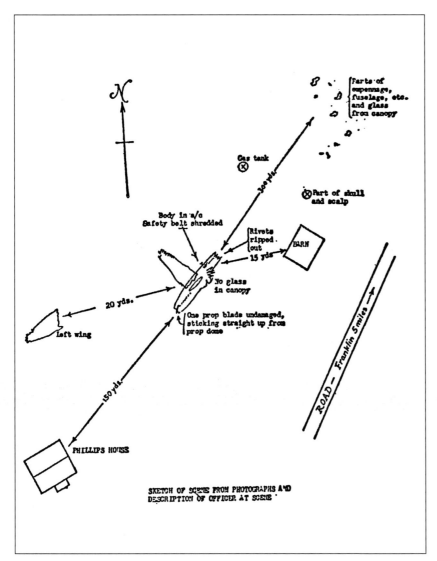

Gas tank
⊗

Parts of empennage, fuselage, etc. and glass from canopy

⊗ Part of skull and scalp

Body in a/c
Safety belt shredded

Rivets ripped out
15 yds

BARN

No glass in canopy

20 yds.

Left wing

One prop blade undamaged, sticking straight up from prop dome

ROAD — Franklin 5 miles

150 yds.

PHILLIPS HOUSE

SKETCH OF SCENE FROM PHOTOGRAPHS AND DESCRIPTION OF OFFICER AT SCENE

Above: *The map of the Mantell crash scene sketched at the beginning of the investigation.*

A second theory stated that the UFO was a large Skyhook weather balloon, then being used for high-altitude experimental flights. Such balloons flew at altitudes in excess of 60,000 feet and had diameters of approximately 100 feet. During the period of this sighting, the Navy was conducting a program utilizing Skyhook balloons. This program was classified at the time, and therefore these flights were known only to those with a "need-to-know" status. Later, it was determined that on the date of the Godman Field sighting, a balloon was released by the Navy from Clinton County Airport in Ohio. Its release time was related to a wind plot for January 7, 1948, which indicated that the balloon would have been in the Godman area at the time of the sighting. ATIC investigators decided that Captain Mantell was attempting to close in on this balloon, which was still more than 40,000 feet above him.

The Air Force concluded in this case that Venus was probably the original cause of the sighting, since the object remained in the area for a long period and was relatively stationary. However, the object pursued by Captain Mantell is widely believed to have been the Skyhook balloon, probably also what was seen by other witnesses, who described the UFO as pear-shaped and metallic.

Because the Navy's Skyhook program was a classified project in 1948, it is understandable that the official statement would not mention a balloon, but would surmise instead that an F-51 pilot met his death chasing Venus to 15,000 feet. Several years later, Air Force Captain Edward Ruppelt at Project Blue Book decided to check this with an evaluation of some fifty-five cross-country balloon tracks. The results were amazing, and not what had been predicted. Tracks were taken from flights made during July and August 1952, when reports of UFO sightings were coming in at the rate of fifty per day. The balloon tracks coincided with the hundreds of reports of flying saucers at only eight points during that two-month period. The inclusion of this startling information in the published report on Project Blue Book is widely overlooked.

Thomas Mantell: An Unsolved Case

Mantell's fatal close encounter remains one of the most mysterious and controversial cases in UFO history. The initial far-fetched Air Force explanation—that Mantell was chasing the planet Venus—was never taken seriously by either pilots or the public. Mantell had reported sighting an object that "appears metallic and of tremendous size," not a distant point of faint light, as Venus appeared on the day of Mantell's death.

The second Air Force explanation, that Mantell had pursued a military Skyhook balloon, also raised more questions than it answered. Both high-atmosphere balloons and UFOs had been sighted in the area by credible witnesses at the time Mantell disappeared. One witness was an astronomer, who said he had observed a cone-shaped object that proved to be a balloon when he viewed it through a telescope. Others simply reported sighting unidentified flying objects.

Later testimony by experts at the Aeronautical Division of General Mills, Inc. in Minneapolis, who had been launching and tracking Skyhook balloons since the late 1940s, indicated that such balloons seemed to attract UFOs. General Mills personnel told Air Force generals in 1952 that they had seen so many UFOs hovering near their balloons that they no longer paid much attention to them. Until Project Grudge was reorganized in 1952, they had simply stopped making UFO reports to the Air Force because of the official attitude of incredulity and dismissal, according to Ruppelt.

Those closest to Captain Mantell attest to his experience and stability. He was a war hero who had been decorated with the Silver Star and the Flying Cross for a dangerous mission behind enemy lines on D-Day. After the war, he operated a civilian flying school and flew fighter planes for the National Guard. His widow, Peggy Mantell, recalled that "He was a fun guy, but a serious guy…Flying was his first love." And a long-time friend and flying partner said of Mantell's last flight, "The only thing I can think was that he was after something that he believed to be more important than his life or his family."

Activating Project Sign

The Mantell incident constitutes one of the most prominent cases in UFO history. As sightings continued, another of the most intriguing, and one that would defy explanation, occurred six months later, on July 23, 1948, near Montgomery, Alabama. An Eastern Airlines DC-3, piloted by Clarence Chiles and John Whitted, veteran World War II pilots, encountered what they would describe as a glowing "aerial submarine" as long as a B-29 Superfortress (99 feet), which circled their aircraft. It reportedly had a dark blue light that quivered across the skin and a double row of what they described as ports or vents along the side emanating white light.

Even before the encounters at Godman Field and Montgomery, the U.S. Air Force had moved to set up a system for evaluating available evidence: Project Sign. It was assigned Project Number XS-304 (January 22, 1948) by authority of a letter from the Deputy Chief of Staff, Matériel, U.S. Air Force. Assistance in analyzing the reported observations had been provided by other divisions of Air Matériel Command in accordance with Technical Instructions TI-2195, dated February 11, 1948, and entitled *Project Sign: Evaluation of Unidentified Flying Objects.*

Analysis of the reported incidents, as an effort to identify astrophysical phenomena, was accomplished by Ohio State University under contract with Air Matériel Command. On July 21, 1948, the Air Force contracted with the Rand Corporation to gather and present information that would help evaluate the

"remote possibility" that some of the observed objects might have been "space ships or satellite vehicles." Rand already had a secret government contract to design a spacecraft and was to provide information on basic design and performance characteristics that might distinguish a possible "space ship."

Members of the Scientific Advisory Board, who reported to the Chief of Staff and provided consulting services to Project Sign, included Dr. Irving Langmuir, Chief of General Electric Research, and Dr. G.E. Valley of the Massachusetts Institute of Technology (MIT). Valley reviewed the reported incidents, grouped the various objects, then analyzed each group from the standpoint of scientific feasibility.

In connection with psychological studies of reporting witnesses being conducted by the AMC Aeromedical Laboratory, extensive investigations of witnesses were carried out. The FBI also "assisted Project Sign in a number of instances, both by investigations of the character and reliability of witnesses of incidents and by providing other investigative services." This in turn led to what is known in UFO folklore as the "Men in Black": the infamous men in black suits who visit UFO witnesses and ask leading and intimidating questions.

Ohio State University contracted with Air Matériel Command to supply astronomical services in an effort to identify meteors, planetoids and associated phenomena. Professor J. Allen Hynek, an Ohio State astrophysicist and head of the University Observatory, was hired as a consultant to Project Sign. Hynek

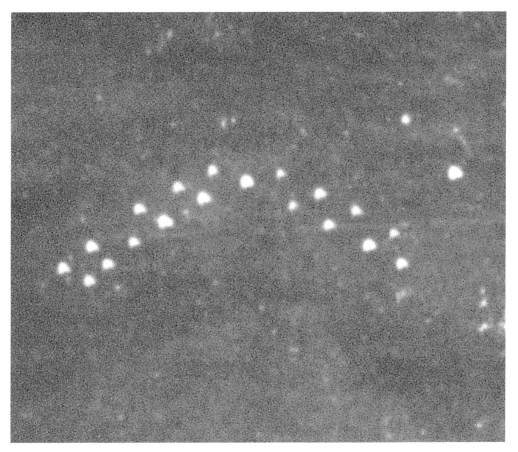

Left: *This object, photographed over Lubbock, Texas, on August 25, 1951, resembles the description in the famous Chiles-Whitted sighting: the double row of white lights they reported is a distinctive characteristic.*

commented early in the evaluation that he was satisfied that a number of the reported observations represented astrophysical phenomena. However, he later became a skeptic, and eventually one of the world's leading exponents of the theory that UFOs had intelligent, extraterrestrial origin.

Project Sign conducted a survey of 243 domestic and 30 foreign UFO sightings, issuing its report on December 16, 1948. Based on the possibility that the objects were unconventional types of aircraft, technical analyses were made to determine the aerodynamic, propulsion and control features that would be required for the UFOs to perform as described in the reports. The objects sighted were grouped into four classifications, according to configuration:

1. Flying discs (very low aspect ratio aircraft)
2. Torpedo- or cigar-shaped bodies with no wings or fins visible in flight
3. Spherical or balloon-shaped objects
4. Balls of light

The first three groups would be capable of flight by aerodynamic or aerostatic means, and might be propelled and controlled by methods known to aeronautical designers. The fourth appeared to have no physical form attached, but the means of support may not have been seen by the observer. Approximately 20 percent of the incidents were identified as conventional aerial objects, to the satisfaction of personnel assigned to Project Sign.

The report considered "the possibility that some of the incidents may represent technical developments far in advance of knowledge available to engineers and scientists of this country," but Project Sign concluded that "No facts are available...that will permit an objective assessment of this possibility. All information so far presented on the possible existence of space ships from another planet or of aircraft propelled by an advanced type of atomic power plant have been largely conjecture. Based on experience with nuclear power plant research in this country, the existence on Earth of such engines of small enough size and weight to have powered the objects described is highly improbable."

Project Sign's report also stated that "no definite and conclusive evidence is yet available that would prove or disprove the existence of these unidentified objects as real aircraft of unknown and uncon-ventional configuration. It is unlikely that positive proof of their existence will be obtained without examination of the remains of crashed objects. Proof of non-existence is equally impossible to obtain unless a reasonable and convincing explanation is determined for each incident."

On the technical side, the report recalled that wind tunnel experiments conducted by the National Advisory Committee for Aeronautics (NACA, the predecessor of NASA) in 1933 had shown that aircraft with circular planform wings (disc-shaped aircraft) "showed both maximum lift coefficients and stall characteristics much more favorable than could be anticipated." In effect, the Air Force had concluded that there was practicality in a disc-shaped aircraft.

Also included in the Sign report was an extensive technical discussion written by Dr. James E. Lipp and submitted by Rand, which analyzed in minute detail the possibility of intelligent life on Mars or Venus, and theorized that the Martians might have been "alarmed by the sight of our A-bomb shots as evidence that we are warlike and on the threshold of space travel." Such a scenario was grist for the grade "B" science-fiction movies of the era, but its inclusion in a scientific government report is amazing.

Lipp also provided a lengthy analysis of possible Martian spacecraft. If Project Sign's intention was to prove that flying saucers could not possibly be from outer space, it failed. If its intention was to encourage popular speculation about extraterrestrial invaders, it succeeded. To make matters worse, the inconclusive report was classified "Secret" and

Below: *Project Sign classified UFOs into four groups according to shape. The first and third groups—discs and spherical or balloon-shaped objects—were the most numerous. This domed object, photographed in Riverside, California, in November 1951, is similar in shape to many of Sign's cases.*

remained so for twelve years. During that time, the bits and pieces that were leaked contributed to an aura of mystery and the belief that the government was hiding something.

Rumors concerning one document in particular augmented this aura of mystery considerably: the Sign intelligence report drafted in August 1948, known as the "Estimate of the Situation." This "rather thick document," according to Ruppelt, "contained the Air Force's analysis of many of the incidents.... All of them had come from scientists, pilots, and other equally credible observers." The report was submitted to Gen. Hoyt Vandenberg, who rejected it forthwith on the grounds of insufficient factual support for its claims: its conclusion was that the most credible evidence indicated extraterrestrial origins for UFOs. Vandenberg ordered that all copies of the report be burned.

The existence of this sensational top-secret document was denied for many years by Air Force sources, including spokesman Lt. Col. Lawrence J. Tacker, who stated in 1960 that it was an invention of "avid saucer believers." Ruppelt, however, had published details in his own account in 1956, and Maj. Dewey Fournet had also confirmed having seen the document. "I studied it," he repeated in a later interview (*UFO Universe*, November 1988). "Naturally," he continued, "anybody in the position such as Vandenberg would say, 'I am not going to sign it'."

It is believed that the Sign staff fell from favor as a result of this report, and only those who stood by more mundane explanations were retained for the new, more conservative, phase of official evaluation.

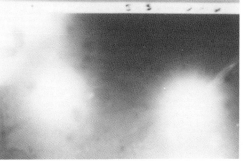

Left: *The fourth of Sign's classifications was balls of light, like these observed over Adak, Alaska, in November 1950.*

The Project Grudge Evaluation

The designation for the U.S. Air Force's Air Technical Intelligence Center (ATIC) investigation of UFOs—Project Sign—was changed to Project Grudge in December 1948 at the request of Brigadier General Donald Putt, Air Force Director of Research and Development. With a new staff, the project went to work on February 11, 1949, collecting and evaluating reports, just as Project Sign had done.

It issued one report, designated Technical Report No. 102-AC 49/15-100, dated August 1949. Originally classified "Secret" and declassified in August 1952, Project Grudge had examined 244 reports and concluded that "Evaluations of reports of UFOs to date demonstrate that these flying objects constitute no threat to the security of the United States."

Professor J. Allen Hynek, the Ohio State astrophysicist who had been a consultant to Project Sign, was retained by Project Grudge. ATIC determined that it would be useful to have an astronomer to (in Dr. Hynek's words) "weed out obvious cases of astronomical phenomena—meteors, planets, twinkling stars, and other natural occurrences that could give rise to the flying saucer reports then being received, and I was a natural choice. I was then director of Ohio State University's McMillin Observatory and as such, the closest professional astronomer" to Wright-Patterson AFB.

Comments from an astronomical point of view by Dr. Hynek predominate in the Project Grudge report. About 32 percent of the cases were considered to have been explained as sightings of astronomical objects. Another 12 percent were judged to have been sightings of weather balloons, on the basis of detailed analysis of reports made by the Air Weather Service and the Air Force Cambridge Research Laboratory. Some 33 percent were dismissed as hoaxes, reports too vague for explanation, or sightings of airplanes under unusual conditions. The remaining 23 percent were considered "unknown."

Project Grudge also recommended, as had the Project Sign report, that the investigation and evaluation of reports of UFOs be reduced in scope. UFO investigation continued on a reduced scale, and in December 1951 the Air Force entered into a contract with a pri-

Below: *A leading scientist in his field, Professor J. Allen Hynek was hired to "weed out obvious cases of astronomical phenomena." Here, a supernova erupts in the Large Magellanic Cloud.*

vate industrial organization for another detailed evaluation of the UFO cases on file. The report, which was completed March 17, 1954, is commonly referred to as "Special Report 14." Reports 1 through 13 were represented by the Air Force to be "progress reports dealing with administration." Special Report 14 reduced and evaluated all UFO data held in Air Force files. Basically, it made the same conclusions as the preceding Sign and Grudge reports.

Throughout the course of Projects Sign and Grudge, the ATIC had collected and analyzed reports of 400 incidents under the supposition that virtually all sightings were due to mass hysteria or "war nerves," hoaxes by persons seeking publicity, reports by "psychopathological" persons, or simply misinterpretations of known objects. However, the evaluations concluded that most of the reports received were *not* due to hysteria, war nerves, hoaxes, publicity seekers and psychopathology. Some were, certainly, but most were accounts from persons who had "definitely seen something that they themselves could not explain at the time of the sighting and have very sincerely made their report to the Air Force."

With the release of the Project Grudge report, the Air Force felt that its Psychological Warfare Division and other related government agencies should be informed of the evaluation results. The Air Force was aware that public concern about the UFO issue could be used in psychological warfare. But overall, between 1949 and 1951 the project was carried out on a low-priority basis. Even though very little pub-

licity had been given to the subject during this time, reports continued to come in. These were mainly from military personnel, and could be classified as "good" reports. To the Air Force, a "good" report was one in which several people were involved and the motives of the witnesses could not be questioned. For the moment, the Air Force was treading water.

Above: *Of the 400 reports evaluated by projects Sign and Grudge, over 10 percent were foreign sightings. This dramatic, low-flying saucer was observed over New Zealand in 1951.*

The McMinnville Case

One of the most memorable sightings in UFO literature occurred at McMinnville, Oregon, on May 11, 1950. While many early sightings have subsequently been revealed as hoaxes, the McMinnville incident has stood the test of time in the minds of many serious UFO researchers. This is especially important insofar as both Project Blue Book and the subsequent Scientific Study of Unidentified Flying Objects (SSUFO) would spend an unusual amount of time and effort on the McMinnville Case.

The sighting occurred in the back yard of the Trents' farm, about a fifth of a mile south of what was then U.S. Highway 99 South (now Oregon State Route 99), but generally known as the Salmon River Highway. Mrs. Trent was feeding rabbits in the yard behind the house at about 7:45 PM when she first sighted a metallic-looking, disc-shaped UFO in the sky. As far as Mrs. Trent could remember when she was interviewed 17 years later, the rabbits gave no indication of disturbance. In one variation on the story, Mrs. Trent called her husband, Paul, and ran into the house to fetch him from the kitchen, although another account states that they had "been out in the back yard," and "both saw it at the same time."

Immediately after they both saw the object—apparently as it was still in a northerly direction, moving slowly toward the west—they located their camera. At this time, "The object was coming in toward us and seemed to be tipped up a little bit. It was very bright—almost silvery—and there was no noise or smoke."

Paul Trent explained that he took the first picture, then wound his film quickly as the object gathered speed and turned toward the northwest. He had to move rapidly to his right to get the second picture, less than 30 seconds after the first. Mrs. Trent ran into the house to call her mother-in-law, got no answer, and returned outside just in time to see the UFO "dimly vanishing toward the west."

In 1967 investigators for the SSUFO interviewed the Trents and examined the photos in detail. They conducted exhaustive studies of the angle and position of the UFO in the photographs and concluded that "the possibility of optical fabrication seems remote. A model thrown into the air by hand appears an unlikely possibility because of the evidence for absence of rotation."

Another possibility was considered. The object appears beneath a pair of wires, so it might have been a model suspended from one of the wires. This possibility is strengthened by the observation that the object appears beneath roughly the same point in the two photos, in spite

Below: *Photographed nine months before the McMinnville sighting, this object over Fairfield-Suisun (now Travis) AFB, California, resembles the Trents' description.*

of their having been taken from two positions. This can be determined from irregularities, or "kinks," in the wires. Given this, SSUFO investigators reported that "One must choose between an asymmetric model suspended from the overhead wire, and an extraordinary flying object....This is one of the few UFO reports in which all factors investigated, geometric, psychological, and physical, appear to be consistent with the assertion that an extraordinary flying object, silvery, metallic, disc shaped, tens of meters in diameter, and evidently artificial, flew within sight of two witnesses. It cannot be said that the evidence positively rules out a fabrication, although there are some physical factors, such as the accuracy of certain photometric measures of the original negatives, which argue against a fabrication."

The Media and UFOs

The subject of mass popular interest in UFOs was a factor in discussion of the phenomena from the beginning, especially in the United States. Newspapers had used the 1947 reports as fodder during the summer's slow news days, and by 1950 magazine and book publishers had discovered that money could be made in the UFO field. The first major magazine article appeared in the issue of *True* magazine dated January 1950. Entitled "The Flying Saucers are Real," it was written by Major Donald E. Keyhoe (USMC, retired). *True* magazine, with its reputation as a sensationalist tabloid, seemed an unusual venue for announcing a major scientific discovery, but this article purported to do so. It unequivocally asserted that flying saucers were vehicles being used by visitors from outer space to scrutinize the Earth. The article stirred up a great deal of media attention.

Keyhoe, a former Marine Corps pilot, wrote that UFOs were crewed by intelligent beings from outer space who had come to observe Earth's people, an idea that dovetailed nicely with Dr. James E. Lipp's outlandish assertions in the Project Sign report. This article and the subsequent attention made Keyhoe an overnight celebrity and brought him a book contract with Fawcett. Keyhoe then took Lipp's notion of intelligent, Earth-studying extraterrestrials a step further by stating that he felt "The U.S. Air Force knew the answer and was hiding it from the public." If the Air Force contributed to the speculation by its secretiveness, any rational attempt to sort out the phenomena was hampered by the popular interest in flying saucers already generated by the media.

In its March 1950 issue, *True* extended its coverage of UFOs with an article entitled "How Scientists Tracked Flying Saucers," written by Commander R.B. McLaughlin (U.S. Navy). McLaughlin came out on the side of the extraterrestrial hypothesis. Describing a UFO he had seen at White Sands Missile Range in New Mexico, he declared, "I am convinced that it was a flying saucer, and further, these discs are spaceships from another planet, operated by animate, intelligent beings."

Interest developed in the mainstream American news media, too. On April 9, 1950, *The New York Times* published an editorial with the headline, "Those Flying Saucers: Are They or Aren't They?"; and *U.S. News and World Report* carried a story in its April 7 issue relating the flying saucers to the Navy's abandoned XF5U-1 project.

By 1950 two important notions were out of the figurative "Pandora's box" of UFO research. Such speculators as Dr. Lipp had been instrumental in giving the world the hypothesis of extraterrestrial origin, and Keyhoe had institutionalized the notion of a government cover-up. A large segment of the public was ready to believe both.

The Project Blue Book Evaluation

After Project Grudge ended in August 1949, official interest in UFOs in the United States was at an ebb. Certainly the urgency of the Korean War, which began in June 1950—and began to go badly for the United States five months later—consumed a great deal of the Air Force's attention in the early 1950s. However, the Air Technical Intelligence Center at Wright-Patterson AFB continued to collect reports of the sightings, under the Project Grudge designation.

With the start of the Korean War, the U.S. Air Force called a great many reservists to active duty. One of them was Captain Edward J. Ruppelt. Assigned to ATIC in January 1951, Ruppelt soon became involved in the center's flying saucer evaluation. The acronym "UFO" did not yet exist, but it would soon be coined by Ruppelt himself. A few hours into the job, Ruppelt discovered that there were numerous credible trained-observer accounts—many from Air Force personnel—but that the "powers that be" didn't believe in UFOs and that the "official reaction was a great big, deep belly laugh."

Ruppelt became a Project Grudge investigator and spent his time debunking the flying saucer reports, while noting the ones that defied explanation. In his 1956 book, *The Report on Unidentified Flying Objects,* he noted that he had encountered many identifiable objects and some clever hoaxes, as well as reports of UFOs by qualified, trained observers that could not be identified, even with all the resources at ATIC's disposal.

Throughout 1951 a growing number of UFO reports were coming in from Air Defense Command (ADC) interceptor pilots, so Captain Ruppelt enlisted the support of ADC commander General Benjamin W. Chidlaw and his director of intelligence, Brigadier General W.M. Burgess. Certainly, ADC interceptor pilots were the kind of trained observers that the Air Force couldn't ignore, so headquarters rethought the lowered priority for the investigation.

Ruppelt summarized the rationale for an ongoing investigation: "The hypothesis that since nothing hostile has been discovered in the past, nothing hostile will be discovered in the future can be followed and the project discontinued. However, with the present-day technological advances, this hypothesis may involve a certain degree of risk in the

Below: *Robert Rinker, a technician at a weather center near Climax, Colorado, said cautiously of this object he photographed in March 1967: "I haven't said it's a flying saucer yet." Meteorologists, like pilots, make highly credible witnesses whose testimony is considered specialist by investigators.*

U.F.O. EVALUATING THE EVIDENCE

Right: A Project Sign-era artist in the U.S. Air Force Air Matériel Command sketched this unexplained object that did not match any of the four shapes most commonly reported.

future." He went on to recommend a continuing and expanded project, commenting that:

1. If the project is to continue it must be expanded in scope. This would require a limited increase both in the amount of funds and of personnel. Reports now being received are not thoroughly analyzed. Many sources of information that are available have not been utilized due to the limited scope of the project. The possibility that any definite conclusions as to the nature of the objects being reported will ever be reached is extremely doubtful under the present operations.

2. At the present time the objects that have been reported apparently present no threat to the United States. However, some time in the future some unfriendly nation might conceivably develop unconventional weapons that would appear similar to the objects that are presently being reported, and it is apparent from the past five years' history of this project that present operations could not adequately cope with such an occurrence.

3. There are still "incredible reports by credible observers" that have not been and should be thoroughly explained.

4. An enemy could use the present flying saucer report as a psychological weapon, and if an organization is not available to cope with such reports (i.e., the mere existence of such an organized project would

be a counter-weapon), a certain degree of panic could result.

5. It is thought possible that all the reports of unidentified flying objects are due to misinterpretation of known objects. The continuance of an expanded project will provide the necessary data to arrive at more definite conclusions as to this possibility.

In March 1952, the UFO research project formerly called Grudge became known as Project Blue Book. No longer an ATIC activity, it was assigned to a separate entity to be known as the Aerial Phenomena Group (APG). From this time until it was officially terminated in 1969, the project concerned itself with investigation of sightings, evaluation of the data and release of information to proper news media through the secretary of the Air Force's Office of Information (SAFOI).

Captain Ruppelt headed Project Blue Book, and his Pentagon liaison was Air Force intelligence officer Captain (later Major) Dewey J. Fournet. During 1952 they would see an unprecedented explosion in UFO sightings.

Below: A U.S. Coast Guard cameraman photographed this formation of brightly glowing objects at Salem, Massachusetts, on July 16, 1952— the month in which the incidence of UFO sightings peaked around the world.

5: The Year of the Saucers

"The continued emphasis on [UFOs threatens] the body politic. We cite as examples the clogging of channels of communication by irrelevant reports, the danger of being led by continued false alarms to ignore real indications of hostile action, and the cultivation of a morbid national psychology in which skillful, hostile propaganda could induce hysterical behavior and harmful distrust of duly constituted authority."

— The Robertson Panel, January 1953

During 1951 moviegoers thrilled to the earliest flying saucer films, still considered classics of the genre. In *The Day The Earth Stood Still*, Michael Rennie played the noble alien opposite Patricia Neal, as a giant disc-shaped craft from another world landed on the Mall in front of the United States Capitol Building. Dozens of "B" movies produced in the 1950s featured disc-shaped and cigar-shaped spacecraft invading Earth under the intelligent control of a strange menagerie of creatures from outer space, but *The Day The Earth Stood Still* remains a cult classic.

Within a year, unfolding events would appear to be life imitating art. The number of UFO reports in 1952 was eight times that for the previous two years, and the sightings would include the amazing—and still unexplained—"attack" on Washington, D.C.

The Momentum Picks Up

Project Blue Book was formed officially in March 1952, and reports continued to trickle in. A major multiple-witness event occurred on April 20, when 20 groups of up to nine objects were observed near Flint, Michigan, by several witnesses on the ground in clear weather. The month of May 1952 saw an unusual concentration of trained-observer sightings across the southern United States. On May 1, near George AFB, California, six discs

Opposite: *The 1950s and '60s were marked by "UFO-mania," especially in the United States. Particularly compelling to the popular imagination were such city-center sightings as this, in mid–1960s Omaha, Nebraska.*

were seen by four witnesses on a clear day. The objects were flying in formation, one of them rotating on its vertical axis. A week after that, about 600 miles east of Jacksonville, Florida, the crew of Pan American World Airways Flight 203, en route from New York to San Juan, Puerto Rico, at 8,000 feet, observed three evenly spaced lights not attached to an airplane pass ahead of them. On the same day, eight airmen in a U.S. Air Force B-36

from Davis-Monthan AFB, Arizona, watched two bright round objects pass them, stop, turn sharply and fly away at high speed.

On May 19, at 18,000 feet over San Angelo, Texas, the crew of an RB-39 (the reconnaissance variant of the B-36) observed seven such objects about 50 miles away. They were flying in tight circles at altitudes ranging from 25,000 to about 6,000 feet. There were important sightings elsewhere in the United States—notably Tremonton, Utah—as well as in Korea, Japan, Europe, North Africa and Australia. One of the most remarkable was on May 7, 1952, at Barra da Tijuca on the coast of Brazil, near Punta da Marisco and Rio de Janeiro.

The Barra da Tijuca sighting was listed in the *Scientific Study of Unidentified Flying Objects* (SSUFO) report as presenting initially "one of the strongest and demonstrably 'genuine' flying saucer sightings." As the SSUFO report points out, the sighting is described in detail in *APRO Special Report No. 1* (Aerial Phenomena Research Organization, Fontes, 1961). According to APRO, the two witnesses, one a press photographer, the other a reporter for *O Cruzeiro* magazine, were on a "routine job" when they saw and photographed a "flying disc." Later, a banker named Fernando Cleto appeared on Brazilian television claiming authorization by Brazilian Air Force officials to show some of their documents on the case that would prove the existence of flying saucers. However, in one of the photos, the disc is clearly illuminated from the left, while the hillside below appears to be illuminated from the right.

The Tremonton "Sea Gulls"

If one were to rate the potential accuracy of UFO reports by the official interest and investigative resources invested in them, then the occurrence of July 2, 1952, would be near the top of the list. U.S. Navy Chief Warrant Officer Delbert Newhouse, his wife and their two children, ages 12 and 14, were en route from Washington, D.C., to Portland, Oregon, when they saw and made home movies of a "rough formation" of UFOs "milling around the sky."

Newhouse was a reliable witness. He had graduated from naval photographic school in 1935, had been in the Navy for 19 years with service as a warrant officer, had logged over 1,000 hours on aerial photography missions and had 2,200 hours as a chief photographer.

It was about 11:10 AM, and the Newhouses were driving north on U.S. Highway 30, seven miles north of Tremonton, Utah. The weather was clear, the visibility good and the winds relatively light. Mrs. Newhouse noticed a group of "bright, shining objects in the air off towards the eastward horizon" that she could not identify. She asked her husband to stop the car and look. There were 10 or 12 objects that bore no relation to anything Newhouse had seen before. They were milling about in a rough formation and proceeding in a westerly direction.

Newhouse got out his 16mm Bell & Howell Automaster movie camera. Loading it hurriedly with Kodachrome Daylight film, he exposed approximately 30 feet of film. There was no reference point in the sky, and it was impossible for him to make any estimate of speed, size, altitude or distance. Then one of the objects reversed course and proceeded away from the main group. Newhouse held the camera still and allowed the

Opposite: *A number of highly publicized sightings were reported from Brazil during the 1950s, including this UFO allegedly photographed from a Brazilian Navy ship off Trinidade Island. The famous O Cruziero photographs of 1952 were eventually discredited by, among others, Professor Hynek: he believed the journalists involved were motivated by the potential monetary rewards.*

Left: *Outtakes from the Newhouse film: footage of his family.*

Right: Official files include frame-by-frame analyses of Newhouse's 75-second footage, which defied convincing explanation as a film of natural or manmade phenomena.

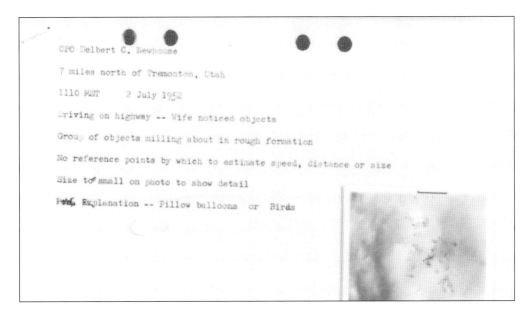

CPO Delbert C. Newhouse

7 miles north of Tremonton, Utah

1110 MST   2 July 1952

Driving on highway -- Wife noticed objects

Group of objects milling about in rough formation

No reference points by which to estimate speed, distance or size

Size too small on photo to show detail

Prob. Explanation -- Pillow balloons or Birds

object to cross the field of view, picking it up again three or four times before all of the objects disappeared.

The film contained about 1,200 frames, or a duration of about 75 seconds. Newhouse had it processed and submitted it to his U.S. Navy superiors. On August 11, he sent the film to Hill AFB, near Ogden, Utah.

The Air Force Project Blue Book team was advised, and they studied the film. The variability of the objects suggested aircraft, but this idea was ruled out because the witnesses heard no engine noise, and a large distance (ten miles) would have indicated improbable speed (1,300 MPH). Balloons were rejected due to the large number of objects, the random milling and the departure of one object from the field. One hypothesis suggested that the objects were sea gulls, but there was no strong evidence in its favor: the objects were too far away, and hence too fast.

Blue Book's Captain Edward Ruppelt reported that after several weeks, "The Air Force photo lab at Wright Field gave up. All they had to say was, 'We don't know what they are but they aren't airplanes or balloons, and we don't think they are birds.'"

Albert M. Chop, the civilian information officer assigned to the Air Technical Intelligence Center, in confirmation of Ruppelt's account, wrote in his assessment: "The ATIC group was convinced they were not aircraft, but could not rule out that the camera might have been slightly out of focus and that the objects were soaring birds."

The film was then forwarded to a group of Navy photo analysts with the Naval Research Laboratory (NRL) at Anacostia Naval Air Station in Anacostia, D.C. The group concluded that the UFOs were intelligently controlled vehicles, not airplanes or birds. They based this conclusion on a frame-by-frame evaluation of the motion and reflected light of the objects, and the changes in light intensity. The analysts stopped short of identifying the objects as interplanetary spacecraft, although this implication was evidently present.

Ruppelt later reported that there was some criticism on the part of the Air Force of the Navy analysts' use of the densitometer: it was suggested that, while Newhouse "thought he had held the camera steady…he could have 'panned with the action' unconsciously, which would throw all of the computations way off. I agreed with this, but I couldn't agree that they were sea gulls."

Robert M.L. Baker, Jr., made an independent evaluation (*Analysis of Photographic Material*, 1955) under the auspices of Douglas Aircraft Company. He ruled out aircraft and balloons for reasons similar to those stated by the Air Force. He also argued against anti-radar chaff (bits of metallic foil) or other airborne debris because of the persistence of non-twinkling "constellations," the small number of objects and the differential motions. It is interesting that Baker included in his evaluation airborne "debris" that was very similar to what had been recovered near Roswell five years earlier. He also ruled out soaring insects, such as "ballooning spiders," since the objects were observed for a short time from a moving car, indicating considerable distance, and there were no observed web streamers.

Baker points out that since the tendency of the observer would be to pan with the object, not against its motion, the derived velocities are lower limits. Thus the suggestion of panning could compound the difficulty with the bird hypothesis. Baker decided that "No definite conclusion could be obtained," as the evidence remained rather contradictory, and no single hypothesis of a natural phenomenon yet suggested seemed to account for the UFO involved.

While the U.S. Navy eventually ruled out the sea gull theory, the U.S. Air Force finally accepted it. Project Blue Book decided that "The visual observations and film are not satisfactorily explained in terms of aircraft, radar chaff, or insects, or balloons, though the film alone is consistent with birds. Observations of birds near Tremonton indicate that the objects are birds, and the case cannot be said to establish the existence of extraordinary aircraft." Ruppelt, however, was among those who remained openly skeptical of the sea gull theory: "Few [witnesses] impressed me as much as Newhouse," he commented. "He didn't just *think* the UFOs were disc-shaped; he *knew* they were.…The question 'What did the UFOs look like' wasn't [even put to him] because when you have a picture of something you don't normally ask what it looks like."

Left: *Albert M. Chop, ATIC's civilian information officer.*

The UFOs Close in on Washington

On July 14, 1952, at 10:12 PM, two Pan American World Airways pilots flying a DC-4 near Norfolk, Virginia, observed eight circular objects over Chesapeake Bay. Their aircraft was at an altitude of 8,000 feet. Some 20 to 25 miles out on the northeast leg of the Norfolk radio beam, six objects were observed below, coming toward the DC-4. When they reached a point slightly below the aircraft, they appeared to roll on edge, and without any radius of turn, shoot off on a heading of about 270 degrees, rolling back into a flat position. Immediately after the change in direction the formation was joined by two other objects.

When first seen, the objects were glowing on the top side with an intense amber-red light more brilliant than the lights of the city below. The pilots thought they resembled a glowing red-hot coal. As they approached the DC-4, they appeared to decelerate just before they changed direction. During their approach they held a good formation, but just before the turn, they appeared to overrun the leader. With deceleration, the glow seemed to dim, and immediately after turning and flattening out, disappeared entirely. The objects reappeared at once, glowing brilliantly again. As they began to climb, the lights went out one by one. They were in view long enough for the pilot to leave his seat after he first observed them, cross the cockpit, pick them up just as they completed their turn and watch them disappear. It was estimated that this took between 10 and 20 seconds.

A possible explanation suggested later was that the objects were actually the fiery afterburners of five jet aircraft that were in the air from Langley AFB, Virginia, about 10 miles southwest of the incident's location. However, the tight formation observed would have been difficult for jets flying at night below 8,000 feet. The almost instantaneous turn could have been some type of illu-

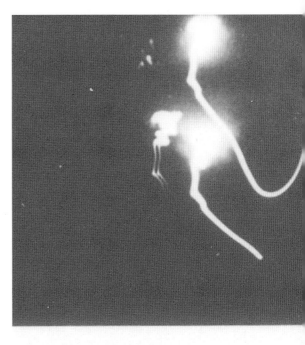

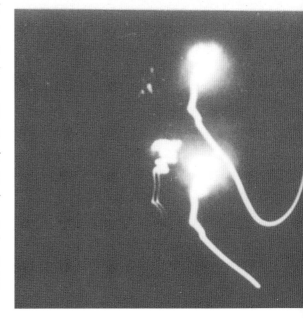

sion. The diminishing light could have been the jets pulling off power before the turn. This, too, is doubtful, since there is no data available on the appearance of the tailpipe of a jet head-on from above. Since there were jet aircraft in the area, it was possible that the Pan American pilots saw them. Therefore, the Air Force officially wrote the incident off as "possibly aircraft."

Near Hampton, Virginia, at twilight on July 16, 1952, Paul Hill, an engineer based at the nearby National Advisory Committee on Aeronautics (NACA) Langley Research Center and other witnesses reported two orange spheres flying side by side toward them from over the Atlantic Ocean. The UFOs were also seen by passengers on a ferry at Old Point, including a U.S. Air Force captain

Left: A few days before the Norfolk, Virginia, sighting, these photographs of unusual aerial phenomena were taken over New York City.

and several "aircraft spotters on duty that night." The spheres then began to circle at high speed. The sighting was reported in the *Newport News Daily Press* with the headline "Flying Saucers over Hampton Roads." A virtually identical sighting occurred three days later in the vicinity of Lavalette, New Jersey, with the pair of spheres reported as orange-yellow to dull red.

Washington "Under Attack"

The film *The Day the Earth Stood Still* was in American theaters during the summer of 1952, when Washington, D.C., was the scene of a flurry of UFO sightings. These incidents, which took place on the nights of July 19–20 and July 26–27, represented the biggest concentration of UFOs in recorded history and convinced a great many people that *these* unidentified objects were real.

The Washington incidents came in the midst of a number of other sightings throughout the eastern United States, especially, as noted above, in the Chesapeake Bay area near Washington. All these events included sightings of glowing objects reported by both ground observers and airline pilots. The objects would also be seen *and* picked up on radar by air traffic controllers at both Washington National Airport and nearby Andrews AFB, which serves the nation's capital.

On radar, these objects were observed to accelerate rapidly from 100 MPH to very high speeds (various estimates ranged from 600 MPH to 7,200 MPH), and to make extremely high-speed turns. Radar operators saw them enter the restricted air space over the White House and the Capitol building, and air control tower personnel watched one hover above the runway at Andrews AFB.

At 11:40 PM on the night of July 19, 1952, air traffic controllers at the Washington, D.C., Air Route Traffic Control (ARTC) Center observed several unidentified "targets" on their VC-2 radar scopes. Eight of the targets were counted and, although an occasional strong return was noted, most of them were classified as fair to weak. After the controllers had checked carefully on the movement (about 100 to 130 MPH) and confirmed their findings with those of Air Search Radar at Washington National Airport, they called Military Flight Service (MFS) and reported it. By now it was about midnight. MFS later told Washington National Airport that the matter should be handled by the nearest military base—Andrews AFB in Maryland.

The targets had been noticed east and south of Andrews AFB, so Washington Center asked the base tower to see if they saw anything, and also asked Andrews approach control to check their radar scopes. Andrews AFB had a man on the roof with binoculars, who spotted an object that looked orange in color and appeared to be hovering in the vicinity.

Soon, commercial pilot reports were received from between Washington and Martinsburg, variously describing lights that moved very rapidly—up and down and horizontally—as well as hovering in one position. One pilot reported being followed to within four miles of touchdown. This was substantiated by Washington National Tower and Washington Center radar.

A conversation between Washington ARTC Center and Andrews AFB ensued, in which the controllers, according to statements in Project Blue Book files: "reached the point where we wondered just how much of this could go on and for how long before something could be done about it....Then another voice came on who identified himself as the combat officer, and said that all the information was being forwarded to higher authority and would not discuss it any further. I insisted I wanted to know if it was being forwarded tonight and he said yes, but would not give me any hint as to what was being done about all these things flying around Washington. He tried to assure me that something was being done about it."

It is curious that these UFOs had timed their joyride to coincide with a period when the interceptors based at Andrews AFB had been temporarily relocated to New Castle County AFB, Delaware, roughly 100 miles to the northeast. Somehow, it took more than two hours for Lockheed F-94 Starfire all-weather interceptors to reach Washington in the early hours of July 20, by which time the

Below: UFOs would be observed over the Capitol dome on numerous occasions during the 1950s, contributing to an atmosphere of Cold-War insecurity.

U.F.O. EVALUATING THE EVIDENCE

UFOs were gone. In the midst of the Korean War, and at a time when Soviet attacks against the United States were considered a real threat, it seems fantastic that Washington, D.C., would have been so poorly protected!

At 1:00 AM on the morning of July 20, a Capital Airlines pilot, Captain Casey Pierman, was in his DC-4 aircraft performing a checklist prior to takeoff from Washington National, when he observed a clear bluish-white light travel from 150 to 10 degrees at a 30-degree angle above the horizon in horizontal flight until it disappeared in the distance. Captain Pierman later told Air Force investigators that he didn't attach any significance to this light until later events demanded attention to it.

Immediately after performing his checklist, Pierman took off from Wash-ington National, climbed to 1,200 feet and switched over from Tower Control to Airway Traffic Control Center (ATCC) at Washington National. At this time, ATCC informed him that their radar scope indicated two or three objects on the screen traveling at high speeds. ATCC instructed Pierman to turn so as to intercept the objects, which were approximately nine miles ahead of him. At this time, the DC-4's rate of climb was roughly 600 feet per minute, and its altitude was between 3,500 and 4,000 feet.

Three to five minutes after takeoff, ATCC informed the pilot that the objects were five miles distant dead ahead. About five seconds later, ATCC told Pierman that the objects were four miles distant dead ahead; three seconds later, they were at 10 o'clock. At this time the pilot reported to ATCC that he plainly saw a DC-4-type aircraft at the 10 o'clock level proceeding in the opposite direction.

Five minutes later, the copilot observed one bluish-white object in a 25-degree dive from northeast to southwest, traveling at a tremendous rate of speed. The copilot told Pierman that he could estimate neither the altitude from which the object began its descent nor the altitude at which it faded. Pierman stated that his altitude was now 6,000 feet, and he could look down almost vertically and see Charles Town, West Virginia.

Next, Captain Pierman and his copilot observed a brilliant bluish-white light reappear where the last light had disappeared and flash past from right to left at approximately 30 degrees above the horizon, traveling at a tremendous rate of speed, apparently outside the Earth's atmosphere. Pierman stated that he may have seen as many as seven objects during as many minutes, but due to the fact

that things were happening so fast he could not keep an accurate account of the number. He told Air Force investigators that in his 24 years as a pilot, he had never seen anything to compare with the objects mentioned in this report. He added that he was convinced the objects were traveling so fast that he would not attempt to estimate their rate of speed.

Harry G. Barnes, the senior radar traffic controller at Washington National that night, later confirmed that Pierman's "descriptions of the movements of the objects coincided with the position of our pips [targets] at all times while in our range." Two hours after Pierman's sighting, four miles from Washington National, the pilot of a Capital Airlines flight reported being followed by a light that was also tracked by radar.

The first notification of these incidents received by Captain Ruppelt came on the morning of July 21: he read it in the Washington papers. An entire day had

Below: *Jet pilots of the 142nd Fighter Interceptor Squadron, summoned to Washington, D.C., from New Castle AFB to investigate the second wave of UFO reports over the nation's capital.*

passed in which he was not informed. He had been at Andrews AFB the previous day and heard nothing. Upon reporting to the Pentagon on the morning of July 22, Ruppelt and Colonel Bower met a Lieutenant Colonel Teaburg, of the Defense Information Estimates Division, who stated that a Captain Berkow, of Headquarters Command at Bolling AFB, was coming in with the report of the incident. This was about 9:00 AM. A half hour later, Berkow arrived and briefed Colonel Bower, Captain Ruppelt, Major Linder of the Air Technical Intelligence Center and others on the incident. He stated that a full report would be delivered to Colonel Bower by the end of the day. During the day several phone calls were received by Captain Ruppelt on the sightings, one from the White House. President Truman's staff was told that an investigation would be made.

On the night of July 26–27, the mysterious UFOs were back in the skies over the nation's capital. This incident involved unidentified targets observed on the radar scopes at the ARTC Center and the tower, both at Washington National Airport, as well as the Approach Control Radar at Andrews AFB. In addition, visual observations were reported to Andrews and Bolling AFB, and to ARTC Center, the latter by commercial pilots and one Civil Aeronautics Administration (CAA) pilot.

Two flights of the Air National Guard F-94 interceptors dispatched from New Castle AFB responded within a half hour, at 11:00 PM. While one F-94 pilot said that he "flew through a batch of radar returns" without spotting anything, the

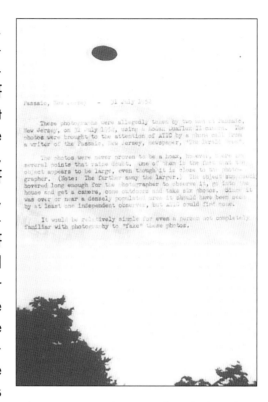

other mentioned seeing four lights, then a single light ahead of him. He was unable to close on it, though, and the light simply "went out."

Varying numbers—up to 12 simultaneously—of unidentified targets were seen on the ARTC radar scope. CAA personnel called them "generally, solid returns," similar to aircraft, but slower. No definable pattern of maneuver was seen except at the very beginning, about 9:50 PM, when four targets in rough line abreast, with about a mile spacing, moved slowly together at an estimated speed of less than 100 MPH on a heading of 110 degrees. At the same time, eight other targets were scattered throughout the scope. ARTC checked Andrews Approach Control by telephone at 10:00 PM and learned that they were also picking up such targets. Unidentified returns were picked up intermittently until about 1:00 AM, after

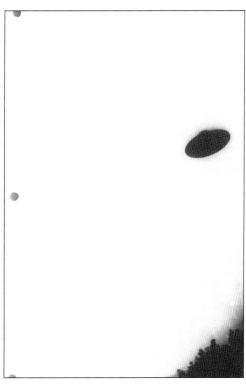

Left: *This sequence was shot during the same week as the Washington sightings in late July 1952, in Passaic, New Jersey, coinciding with a cluster of reports along the Eastern Seaboard.*

which weak and sporadic (unsteady) returns were picked up intermittently for another three hours. The Washington National Tower radar crew reported only one target positively unidentified. This return was termed a "very good target" that moved across the scope from west to east at about 30 to 40 MPH.

The radar operators stated that there could have been other unidentified targets on their scopes, particularly outside their area of aircraft control, which they would not have noticed or would have assumed to be aircraft under ARTC Center control. However, they noticed no other unusual (*i.e.,* very slow, weak or erratic) returns.

ARTC Center controllers also reported that the pilot of the CAA flight had reported at 10:46 PM that he had visually spotted five objects giving off a light glow ranging from orange to white. His altitude at the time was 2,200 feet.

During the evening, commercial pilots reported visuals ranging from "cigarette glow" (red-yellow) to "a light."

One ARTC controller worked with a U.S. Air Force B-25 for about an hour and 20 minutes. This B-25 was vectored in on numerous targets and commented that each vector took him over a busy highway or intersection.

At 11:30 PM Lt. William Patterson, one of the pilots in the second group of interceptors, reported an apparently hostile encounter. Flying into Washington airspace, he saw a cluster of glowing objects ten miles away. When he started chasing the objects, they raced toward him suddenly, and he found himself surrounded. Never having seen anything like this, Patterson nervously asked the radar operators for advice, but they could offer none. Moments later, the UFOs accelerated away from Lt. Patterson's jet and disappeared.

Air Force Captain Dewey Fournet and Navy Lieutenant Holcomb, both assigned to the Air Force Office of Intelligence, arrived at ARTC Center about 12:15 AM. Lieutenant Holcomb observed the scopes and reported "seven good, solid targets." He made a quick check with the airport weather station and determined that there was a slight temperature inversion from the surface to about 1,000 feet. However, he felt that the scope targets at that time were not the result of this inversion, and so advised the command post, with the suggestion that a second intercept flight be requested.

The second intercept flight was summoned from New Castle and controlled by ARTC, but no strong targets remained when the F-94 crews arrived. Fournet and Holcomb remained in ARTC Center until 4:15 AM, but no additional strong targets were picked up through the remainder of the night.

Right: *Major Dewey Fournet was the liaison in the Pentagon for UFO reports for the Air Technical Intelligence Center. He had gained considerable air technical experience during World War II; after the war, when he was in charge of investigating Japanese air crashes; and during the Korean War.*

The ARTC Center radar crew and controllers consisted of trained observers, CAA employees with varying levels of experience. All were reported by Air Force intelligence investigators to be "serious, conscientious and sincere, although somewhat vague about details of their experience on July 26–27."

The ARTC crew commented that, as compared with unidentified returns picked up in the early hours of July 20, these returns appeared to be more haphazard in their actions: they did not follow aircraft, nor did they cross the radar scope consistently, on the same general heading. Some commented that the returns appeared to be from objects "capable of dropping out of the pattern at will," and also that returns had a "creeping appearance."

One member of the crew commented that one object to which an F-94 was vectored just "disappeared from scope" shortly after the plane started pursuing it. All crew members were emphatic that most unidentified returns were "solid." Finally, it was mentioned that unidentified returns had been picked up from time to time over the previous few months, but never before had they appeared in such quantities over such a prolonged period and with such definition.

In a Washington press conference—the largest Air Force press conference since World War II—Major General James A. Samford, intelligence chief, attributed the sightings to a "temperature inversion." But the evidence shows that the Washington incidents are among the largest and strangest series of UFO sightings ever reported.

Calling Captain Ruppelt

T he Washington sightings created a media sensation. "Besides trying to figure out what [they] were," Ruppelt wrote, "we had the problem of what to tell the press. They were now beginning to put on a squeeze by threatening to call a congressman—and nothing chills blood faster in the military."

At 11:30 PM on the night of July 27, 1952, a man identifying himself as a Washington newspaper reporter called Captain Edward Ruppelt. Ruppelt told the caller that he could make no statement for the press—all such statements had to come from the Public Information Office in Washington. The alleged journalist was, however, insistent, and indignant about the fact that he had received the "runaround" all afternoon. He asked whether or not the Air Force had received a report about the Washington UFO sighting that had occurred on the night of July 26. Told that the Air Force had been told of the sighting but could make no comment, the caller said that he believed the Air Force was withholding information that was vital to the public.

The reporter went on to ask what possible causes may have explained the radar returns of the previous night. Ruppelt said again that he had nothing further to say about the Washington sighting, although, as had been announced previously in the press, he could confirm that ATIC had reports of radar sight-ings: he would make no further comment on them. Since there had been a radar pickup there must be something there, the journalist pressed. Ruppelt replied that it was a well-known fact that radar images could be caused by weather, birds, malfunctions in the radar set, interference from other sets and many other reasons.

Asked when the Air Force would have an evaluation on the incident, Ruppelt declined to comment once more. The caller then enquired as to Ruppelt's affiliation with Project Blue Book. Ruppelt referred him to a *Look* magazine article on the project, and told him that no further details would be made available at that time.

UFOs Over Korea and Japan

It is useful to note that waves of UFO sightings have occurred in the context of larger geopolitical events. UFO sightings may have been more prevalent during the Cold War, but what about hot wars? The level of intensity in UFO activity noted during 1952 in the United States—notably in the Washington, D.C., area—was paralleled by a wave of activity in Korea during the Korean War. The conflict lasted from June 1950 through July 1953 and was characterized by intense air combat, long after the ground war devolved into a stalemate in 1951. Until November 1950, the United Nations—mainly United States—forces held unquestioned air superiority. This took a turn when the Chinese entered the war with overwhelming numerical strength on the ground. In the air, the Chinese had large numbers of the Soviet-built Mikoyan-Gurevich MiG-15 jet fighter, which was superior to any American aircraft then in Korea. The U.S. Air Force countered by introducing the North American Aviation F-86 Sabre Jet. For the balance of the war, Sabres and MiGs battled for superiority over Korea with almost daily massed air battles.

As early as September 1950, a U.S. Navy aircraft over Korea had encountered radio interference at the same time that two flat discs were observed. The Navy flight crews noted that "the objects suddenly seemed to halt, back up and begin a jittering, or fibrillating motion.... The objects had a silvered mirror appearance, with a reddish glow surrounding them. They were shaped somewhat like a 'coolie's hat,' with oblong ports from which emanated a copper-green colored light, which gradually

Below: The F-4U was one of the American aircraft involved in the sightings over Korea. On June 20, 1952, a group of Navy F-4U pilots saw a 15-foot oval-shaped UFO in full daylight.

shifted to pale pastel-colored lights and back to the copper-green again." (UFO researcher Richard F. Haines notes that there is a close similarity between this description and that given by a commercial airline flight crew over Lake Michigan on July 4, 1981.)

In the fall of 1951, at least 14 U.S. Navy ground and airborne radar sites tracked a UFO for seven hours as it circled the ships at sea off Korea. The object reportedly moved at speeds ranging from "slow" to over 1,000 MPH and at an altitude of 5,000 feet.

The major wave of sightings in Korea, as elsewhere, seems to have been concentrated in 1952. As Richard Haines points out, descriptions of the UFOs involved during the summer—the same period as the Washington, D.C., sight-ings—were very consistent. Generally, they were described as flat ovals, larger than the MiG-15, which was 36 feet long with a wing span of 33 feet.

At about 11:00 PM on January 29, 1952, three enlisted crew members of a U.S. Air Force B-29 bomber reported a five-minute encounter with a light-orange sphere that flew in formation with one B-29 for about five minutes, then with another B-29 half an hour later. These sightings were similar to those that would occur later in 1952 in the Hampton, Virginia/Langley AFB, area outside of Washington, D.C. The U.S. Air Force offi-cer in charge of press briefings, Captain Dewey Fournet, stated that "the sightings mentioned, although of a different nature, as is usual, are not abnormal occurrences in the combat theater."

Above: *USAF "Starfire" F-94s were widely used in efforts to intercept UFOs reported during the Cold War era, particularly by pilots serving in Korea.*

A month later, near the Chinese border, aircrews reported a cylindrical object with a bluish exhaust plume, but it was nearly midnight and very dark. The object may have been an aircraft other than a MiG that was operating in Chinese airspace and hence off-limits to American aircraft.

At the time of the sightings over the Korean Peninsula, several notable UFO reports came from U.S. military bases in Japan, just a few hundred miles distant. On March 29, 1952, a clear, bright day, an F-84 interceptor pilot saw a small, slivery disc maneuvering 30–50 feet from him, north of Misawa, Japan. The discs "rocked back and forth in 40 degree banks" while moving forward slowly.

Right: During the 1952 wave of sightings, an extraordinary number of reports were substantiated by radar evidence. This episode occurred in Osceola, Wisconsin, during the last week of July.

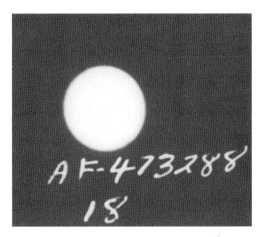

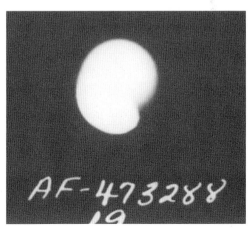

In April, at Kadena AB, Okinawa, Twentieth Air Force ground crews and flight crews on the ground saw a lighted object fly over the base late at night. Its aircraft-like flight path suddenly changed to high-speed maneuvering. It then accelerated—silently—to over 1,000 MPH and flew away.

This speed—faster than that of any contemporary fighters—was observed in similar UFO incidents reported in Korea on the evening of May 15, first by the pilot of an F-51 on a ground support mission, and nearly two hours later by two F-86 pilots. The F-51 pilot described the UFO as a silver object about 50 feet in diameter. At 3:20 AM on May 26, the crew of an F-94 interceptor observed a UFO at 3,000 feet—both visually and on APG-33 radar. They estimated it as traveling at more than 6,400 MPH, far beyond the capability of even the fastest aircraft of today. The official Air Force explanation at the time was that the sighting was due to faulty radar, but Project Blue Book concluded later that the object was a weather balloon. On May 31, another F-94 achieved a radar "lock-on" to a similar object, which appeared to ground observers as a bluish-white light.

The summer of 1952 brought a number of daylight sightings. On June 20, U.S. Navy F4U-4B pilots on a ground-attack mission saw a white or silver oval about 15 feet in diameter. Three days later, a U.S. Air Force fighter bomber pilot reported seeing a black disc-shaped object some seven times wider than it was thick at 12,000 feet, descending "rather irregularly" to 6,000 feet, where it approached the observer to within 1,500 feet before disappearing into the clouds.

Near midnight on August 5, at Haneda AFB, Japan (now Tokyo's Narita Airport), four control tower operators with binoculars observed a brilliant UFO maneuvering over Tokyo Bay. They watched the object hover and then accelerate to 345 MPH, while ground radar tracked it. An F-94 interceptor locked its radar on the UFO for 90 seconds and chased it into a turn, before the object zoomed away.

On the evening of August 9, a U.S. Marine Corps pilot observed a "strange, non-conventional aircraft" passing him at a distance of 1,500 feet. It "had a ball of fire at the rear with a very long streamer of flame...which did not resemble a jet exhaust." In August and September, other "cigar-shaped" objects with "streamers of flame" were observed by Air Force and Navy aircrews over North Korea, but these were officially interpreted as enemy surface-to-air missiles.

During the Korean War, T-6 training planes were used as armed observation aircraft: slower than jets, they afforded good views of the ground action. Among the observations made by T-6 crews in the autumn of 1952 were UFOs. On the morning of October 16, one crew saw a circular, silvery aircraft that "did not appear to have any aerodynamic features." It was moving against the clouds and hovering low among hills. At about 1:00 PM on November 15, the crew of a T-6 flying near Pyongyang, North Korea, sighted a low-flying silver disc about nine feet in diameter.

Among the most spectacular of the 1952 sightings was one that occurred on December 29 over northern Japan. An F-94 interceptor was dispatched to investigate a UFO report from a B-29 crew. Flying at 35,000 feet, the pilot of the interceptor, Wing Commander Colonel D. J. Blakeslee, a World War II fighter ace, reported visual contact. He described the object as having rotating red, green and white lights and three fix beams of white light. Blakeslee applied full power to chase the UFO at over 500 MPH, but it eluded him. Five minutes later it reappeared, this time flying parallel with the F-94. Again Blakeslee tried to close on it, but within five seconds it had sped out of sight. On January 9, 1953, another interceptor reported a similar encounter with a UFO showing rotating lights.

Above: *A frame from a film of a UFO sighted over the Caribbean Sea on November 21, 1952.*

The Royal Air Force Sightings

U.S. Air Force pilots were not the only military airmen who encountered UFOs during 1952. At about 10:35 AM on September 19, during the NATO training exercise "Operation Mainbrace," two British Royal Air Force officers and three other air crewmen watched a UFO following a Gloster Meteor jet fighter heading for RAF Dishforth in Yorkshire. The weather was clear when the circular, white-silver object appeared at about 10,000 feet, flying on the same course as the Meteor. Some observers thought it might be the engine cowling of the Meteor falling from the sky; others thought it resembled a parachute. However, the UFO maintained a slow forward speed for a few seconds before starting to descend. When the Meteor began its final approach, the object seemed to follow it, then stopped and began rotating and "flashing in the sunshine." It moved to the west at high speed, turned and disappeared.

Flight Lieutenant John Kilburn, one of the witnesses, reported that "it was a solid object. We realised very quickly that it could not be a broken cowling or parachute. There was not the slightest possibility that the object we saw was a smoke ring, or was caused by vapour trail from the Meteor or from any jet aircraft. We are also quite certain that it was not a weather observation balloon. The speed at which it moved away discounts this altogether. It was not a small object which appeared bigger in the conditions of light. Our combined opinion is that...it was something we had never seen before in a long experience of air observation."

An official report was sent to the Commander-in-Chief, Air/East Atlantic (a NATO command post), the Chief of the Air Staff (Operations), the Secretary of State for Air and the Air Ministry's Scientific Intelligence Branch. This multiple-witness, highly documented incident caused the "RAF to officially recognize the UFO," it is claimed. Only a month before, Prime Minister Winston Churchill had requested an Air Ministry report on the Washington sightings. The reply stated that the U.S. intelligence briefing had confirmed natural or conventional explanations for all such reports other than deliberate hoaxes.

A little over a year later, on the morning of November 3, 1953, near RAF West Malling in Kent, Flying Officer T.S. Johnson and navigator Flying Officer G. Smythe were flying a two-seat de Havilland NF-10 Vampire night-fighter at 20,000 feet, when they observed a circular, brightly lit object hovering at a higher altitude. It then moved toward them at high speed before disappearing suddenly. The event was reported to their station commander, Group Captain P. Hamley, who, in turn, sent a report up the chain of command to RAF Fighter Command Headquarters.

On December 16, an RAF Fighter Command directive was issued outlining a mandatory procedure for UFO reporting. It was classified "Restricted" and read in part: "personnel are not to communicate any information about phenomena they have observed, unless officially authorised to do so." Like the United States, the U.K. was concerned about national security.

The Robertson Panel: A Rush to Judgment?

The Project Blue Book evaluation gave no indication of a threat to national security, and no evidence that UFOs could have extraterrestrial origins, but the sightings continued to be reported.

Aside from the mystery and potential threat posed by UFOs, there were other concerns. In the wake of the sightings over Washington in 1952, some Defense Department personnel began to worry about public interest in UFOs from a different viewpoint—namely, the possibility that military-communication channels might be jammed with sighting reports at a time when an enemy was launching a sneak attack on the United States. It seemed a real possibility that an enemy (specifically, the Soviet Union), prior to launching such an attack, might generate a wave of UFO reports with the deliberate intention of jamming military-communication channels. The CIA under-

took to assess the situation with the assistance of a special panel of five scientists who had distinguished themselves in physics research and in their contributions to military research during and after World War II.

Against the backdrop of potential hysteria and the increased volume of reports, a Scientific Advisory Panel on UFOs was established by the U.S. government late in 1952. The Democratic Party had just lost the White House—for the first time in 20 years—and there was concern about tying up loose ends before the new Eisenhower Administration was sworn in on January 20, 1953.

The panel would be known informally as the Robertson Panel, for its chairman, the late Professor H.P. Robertson of the California Institute of Technology (Caltech). In a series of meetings and interviews held between January 14 and 18, 1953, "all available data" was examined. Captain Edward Ruppelt of Project Blue Book and U.S. Navy analysts from the Naval Research Laboratory gave briefings, and CIA interest in UFOs was reviewed.

In retrospect, the actions of the Scientific Advisory Panel on UFOs can be compared to those of the Warren Commission investigation of the assassination of John F. Kennedy 11 years later. The Warren Commission was accused of a "rush to judgment," a hurried examination primarily of facts that supported the foreseen conclusion. Having dashed through the material in just four days—with two-hour lunch breaks—the Robertson Panel concluded that UFOs did not threaten the national

Left: Justice Earl Warren, head of the panel that was convened to investigate the assassination of President John F. Kennedy. Like the Robertson Panel members, staff of the Warren Commission experienced political pressure to "solve the case"—and quickly.

Above: *"Colossus," the World War II intelligence computer designed by Alan Turing at England's Manchester University. Professor Robertson had worked extensively with Allied research and intelligence scientists in wartime England.*

security of the United States and recommended that the "aura of mystery attached to the project" be removed.

Another similarity between this panel and the Warren Commission was the fact that the panelists were clearly qualified and competent: their scientific credentials were beyond reproach. Professor Robertson, the chairman, had been a member of the Mathematics Department of Princeton University from 1928 to 1947, when he joined the faculty at the California Institute of Technology. He had distinguished himself by his research in cosmology and the theory of relativity. During the war, he made important contributions to operational research for the Allied forces in London. He then served as research director of the Weapons Systems Evaluation Group in the office of the Secretary of Defense (1950 to 1952), and from 1954 to 1956 he was scientific advisor to the Supreme Allied Commander in Europe.

Professor Samuel A. Goudsmit was another distinguished panelist. In 1925, as a young student in Leyden, the Netherlands, he had discovered electron spin with Professor George Uhlenbeck. Soon after, both came to the University of Michigan, where they developed an influential school of theoretical physics. Goudsmit is also known for having been scientific chief of the Alsos Mission, late in World War II. This intelligence group was sent to Germany to find out what the Germans had accomplished in their effort to produce nuclear weapons. After the war, Goudsmit served on the physics staff of the Brookhaven National Laboratory on Long Island, New York.

Luis Alvarez was a professor of physics at the University of California, Berkeley, and was later vice-president of the American Physical Society. During World War II, he worked with the Radiation Laboratory at the Massachusetts Institute of Technology, where he made an outstanding contribution to development of a microwave radar system for guiding plane landings in heavy fog. In the latter part of the war, he served under J. Robert Oppenheimer on the team that developed the first atomic bomb at Los Alamos National Laboratory, New Mexico. In the postwar period, Alvarez made significant research contributions in high-energy physics. Later, he was involved in using cosmic-ray absorption to seek undiscovered inner chambers in the Egyptian pyramids near Cairo.

Lloyd Berkner had been an engineer with the Byrd Antarctic Expedition during 1928–30. During the prewar period, he was a physicist in the Department of Terrestrial Magnetism of the Carnegie Institution of Washington. Early in the war, he became head of the radar section of the Navy's U.S. Bureau for Aeronautics, then served as executive secretary of the Research and Development Board of the Department of Defense. In 1949 he was special assistant to the secretary of state, and director of the Foreign Military Assistance Program. From 1951 to 1960, Berkner was active in managing the affairs of Associated Universities, Inc., which operates Brookhaven National Laboratory, and eventually became its president. In 1960 he organized and directed the new Graduate Research Center of the Southwest in Dallas, Texas. A long-time member of the U.S. Naval Reserve, he rose to the rank of rear admiral. The concept of an International Geophysical Year (1957–8)—a milestone in international scientific cooperation—was his brainchild.

Professor Thornton Page, a professor of astronomy at Wesleyan University, had done research on the design of underwater ordnance and operations research on naval weapons during World War II. In 1968 he became vice-president for astronomy of the American Association for the Advancement of Science.

It might have been possible to put together other panels that would have performed as well, but it would have been scarcely possible to choose one superior in scientific knowledge, background of military experience and soundness of overall judgment. Why they concluded as they did remains a mystery.

The Robertson Panel report was originally classified "Secret," and was not declassified until the summer of 1966, 13 years later. Only then did the public learn the panel's conclusions: that "the evidence presented on Unidentified Flying Objects shows no indication that these phenomena constitute a direct physical threat to national security. We firmly believe that there is no residuum of cases which indicates phenomena which are attributable to foreign artifacts capable of hostile acts, and that there is no evidence that the phenomena indicate a need for the revision of current scientific concepts." The panel concluded further that "the continued emphasis on the reporting of these phenomena does, in these perilous times, result in a threat to the orderly functioning of the protective organs of the body politic."

Below: *Physics professor and Robertson panelist Luis Alvarez had served on the distinguished team that developed the first atomic bomb, which was headed by J. Robert Oppenheimer (left), seen here with computer consultant John von Neumann.*

6: The Blue Book Era

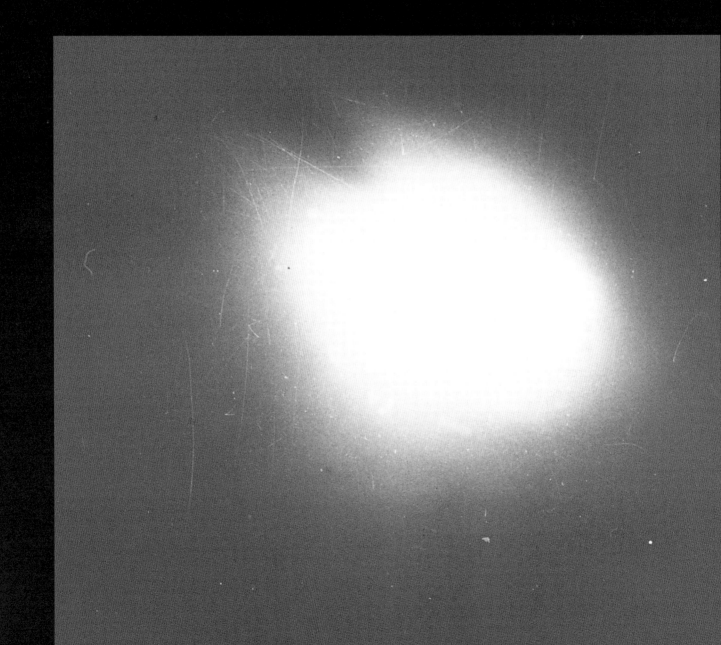

> **"The study of UFOs is a necessity for the sake of world security in the event we have to prepare for the worst in the space age, irrespective of whether we become the Columbus or the Indians."**
>
> — Air Commodore J. Salutun, former secretary of the National Aerospace Council of the Republic of Indonesia, on UFO sightings of the 1950s and '60s.

Both official and civilian evaluation of UFOs would mature during the 1950s and '60s. The period 1947–52 had seen a sense of urgency that assumed an imminent explanation. By 1953 it was becoming apparent that UFOs would continue to defy explanation, perhaps indefinitely. Under Captain Edward Ruppelt, the U.S. Air Force's Project Blue Book continued to collect reports, despite the fact that the government's Scientific Advisory Panel on UFOs had described this activity as "the cultivation of a morbid national psychology."

Ruppelt and Company

Ruppelt and his small staff judged many of the reported sightings explainable, but others defied solution. After the extraordinary wave of 1952, sightings continued around the world. Notable U.S. sightings included one on February 4, 1953, when two white UFOs moving erratically were observed near Yuma, Arizona, by an experienced theodolite tracker who was tracking a balloon at 6,000 feet. On May 14, 1954, in the vicinity of Dallas, Texas, two U.S. Marine Corps aircraft flying at 18,000 and 42,000 feet observed 16 white UFOs at 32,000 feet: suddenly, they turned orange and moved quickly to the north.

Less than a month later, on June 11, astronomer Dr. H. Percy Wilkins—best remembered for his work in lunar observation—was flying in a twin-engine Convair from Charleston, West Virginia, to Atlanta, when he saw two metallic objects flying in and out of the clouds. He reported that they "looked exactly like polished metal dinner plates reflecting the sunlight as they flipped and banked around beside the clouds. Presently a third object came slowly out of a huge cloud, remaining motionless in a shadow of the cloud and therefore darker than the others. Presently it zipped

Opposite: A mysterious "ball of light" photographed over Mooresville, North Carolina, on November 16, 1966—one of the many images on the Project Blue Book Files that cover 10,147 sightings in all.

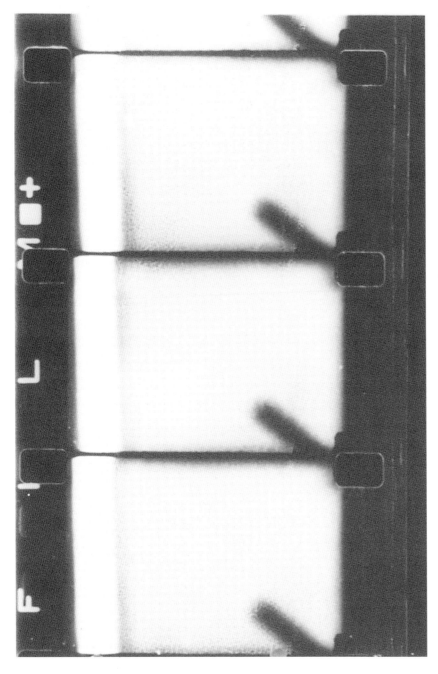

Above: *An early Blue Book case: gun-camera film footage from Victorville, California, recorded on February 2, 1953.*

away and plunged into another cloud mass. After about two minutes, the first two did the same maneuver and I did not see them again."

In some cases, reports slipped through the investigative cracks. On August 28, 1954, numerous witnesses in Oklahoma City—and reportedly, radar operators as well—saw 15 small objects flying in triangle formation, followed by what

appeared to be U.S. Air Force interceptors. No statement from the aircrews is known to have been taken.

Sightings continued in Europe during the 1950s, too. On August 25, 1954, near Birmingham, England, a former Royal Navy Volunteer Lieutenant Commander saw about a dozen luminous objects flying from the north to south. On November 17, throughout England, numerous objects were observed on radar flying from east to west in gradually changing formations. Eleven days earlier, similar formations of objects had been observed visually over Rome. This sighting was accompanied by reports of long filaments falling to the ground. In August, in the vicinity of Pisa, Italy, witnesses reported a large object accompanied by six smaller UFOs.

On June 7, 1957, a group of sightings that were apparently similar in scope to those that had occurred over the Washington, D.C., area in 1952 was reported off the coast of New Jersey. More than 100 UFOs were detected by radar to be fast approaching America's eastern seaboard. The event was sufficiently serious to cause the Air Defense Command (ADC) to scramble three squadrons of interceptors from McGuire AFB. When the aircraft returned after the intercept, the Air Force said only that the objects had been "temporarily" unidentified. No further details were released.

Another New Mexico Balloon
Six years after the legendary 1947 Roswell Incident, which was officially written off as a weather balloon, another

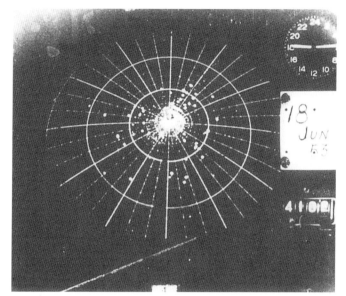
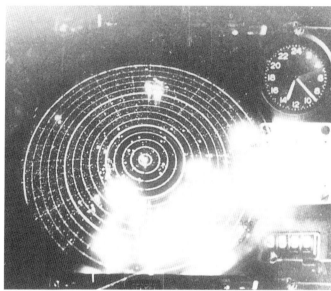

Above: *Radar images of a UFO over Iwo Jima on June 18, 1953, a year during which sightings were reported from all continents.*

"New Mexico balloon" incident occurred. At about 9:15 PM on January 26, 1953, an airman stationed at the U.S. Air Force 769th ACW Squadron radar station at Continental Divide, New Mexico (elevation 7,500 feet), observed a "bright reddish-white object" about 10 miles west of the radar site and approximately 2,000 feet above the ground.

The radar "painted" a strong, steady return at a range of nine miles and about 2,500–7,500 feet above the surface. The weather included a high, thin overcast sky, low scattered clouds, and very good visibility. The object was seen visually—and captured by radar—to have passed behind a nearby hill and reappeared, heading north at about 10–15 MPH. It then moved to the west at 12–15 MPH, to a point 18 miles from the radar site, when it turned north for about 10 miles, before turning back toward the station. Radar and visual contact was lost near the area where it was first detected. Before disappearing, however, it seemed to shrink in size and fade in color to a dull red.

One of the first theories was that the object was a lighted weather balloon (then in use for obtaining data on upper winds). This explanation was rejected by Air Force investigators for two reasons. First, the sighting occurred an hour and 15 minutes after the scheduled release of a Winslow, Arizona balloon, the only one that seemed likely to have shown up in the sighting area, and the balloon should have burst by then, since they generally burst at 30,000 feet, roughly 25 minutes after the Winslow balloon's launch. Secondly, its direction of movement was, at times, directly opposite to the reported upper westerly winds. (The problem of the observed direction of movement cannot be completely resolved, because it depends largely on an analysis of winds in the lower atmosphere, that is, on a scale smaller than ordinarily analyzed on synoptic weather maps.)

Neither of these reasons is sufficient to discount the balloon theory. Weather balloons are often released later than the scheduled time, and this possibility

Blue Book Gallery I

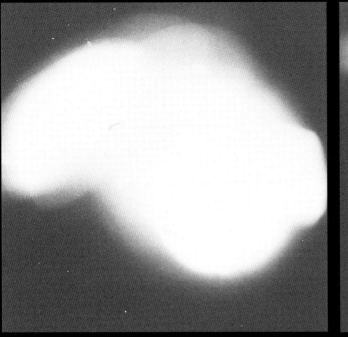

Some of the many and varied unexplained phenomena sighted around the world during the Blue Book years. This page, above: two sightings during December 26, 1960—January 9, 1961, of an object near Buffalo, New York; bottom, July 24, 1957, Norway. Opposite page, clockwise from top left: May 1962, Argentina; July 1959, Switzerland; an object seen on March 31, 1961, over Japan; and September 1, 1957, Chitose, Japan.

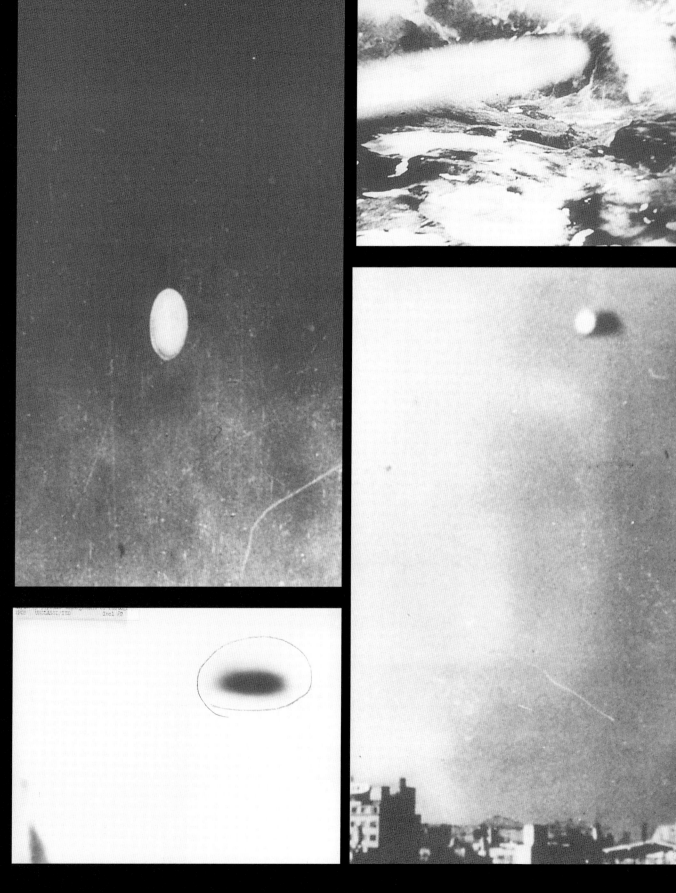

was apparently overlooked. Further, such balloons often leaked and consequently rose at a slower rate than normal. The Winslow balloon might have had so little buoyancy that it could have been caught in local updrafts or downdrafts, and carried by the wind at such a rate that it would be lost from its launch station's sight before it reached burst altitude. On January 27, Winslow listed a "missing" balloon, and some researchers have construed that this was the object observed the night before by the 769th ACW.

The Labrador Sighting
On June 29, 1954, a British Overseas Airways Corporation (BOAC) Boeing 377 Stratocruiser, piloted by Captain James Howard, was en route from New York to London via a refuelling stop at Goose Bay, Labrador. Except for a broken layer of cloud, the sky was clear and the visibility excellent as Howard crossed the Canadian border.

At 9:05 PM local time, Captain Howard and his copilot, Lee Boyd, became aware that something was moving below the thin cloud cover, about five miles to their left at 8,000 feet. As the aircraft passed over the Labrador coast, the cloud lifted and the sun was low in the sky, making for excellent visibility.

Howard then saw the object at his altitude, now flying on a parallel course at his speed. The object resembled an inverted pear and was accompanied by a formation of six smaller "globular" objects. They all appeared to have hard edges and an opaque, gray color, without visible flames or lights. Howard and his crew carefully studied and sketched them for several minutes: they "were strung out in a line, sometimes three ahead and three behind the large one, sometimes two ahead and four behind, and so on, but always at the same level." Howard also noted that "the large object was continually, slowly, changing shape in the way that a swarm of bees might alter its appearance."

After ten minutes of careful observation, Captain Howard called Goose Bay, now just within radio range, to ask if other aircraft were nearby. Upon hearing the reply "no other traffic in your area," Howard then reported his sighting, and Goose Bay vectored an F-94 to investigate. The objects continued to pace the Stratocruiser for about 84 miles, about 20 minutes in all, affording its crew and many of its 30 passengers an unusually close-range view.

During the wait for the interceptor's arrival, the UFO started to change its shape "into what looked like a flying arrow—an enormous delta-winged plane turning in to close with us," as Howard described it. Continuing to change, the object appeared to flatten and elongate and, simultaneously, to close in and recede, while the smaller globes continued maneuvering about the large object.

As the F-94 approached, its pilot asked Howard to confirm a description and location for the UFOs, when the small objects abruptly vanished, apparently inside the large one. Howard then saw the UFO zoom away, receding to a pinpoint in mere seconds, before it vanished completely.

Left and below:
Aerial views showing the Labrador area in similar visibility conditions to those on the evening of June 29, 1954, when a UFO appeared to track a BOAC flight headed for Goose Bay (below, at top right) for a full 20 minutes.

U.F.O. EVALUATING THE EVIDENCE

Right: When Captain James Howard and his crew were questioned by USAF intelligence at Goose Bay, their unusual sighting was met without apparent surprise. A number of UFO sightings had been reported in the area, and the phenomenon continued through the 1950s and '60s. This dramatic, cometlike UFO was photographed from Melville Air Station, Labrador, on August 5, 1963.

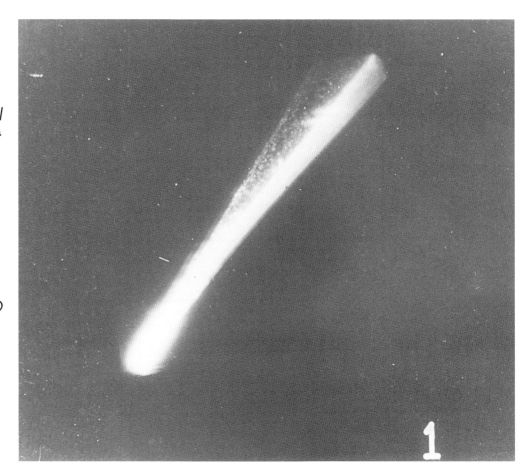

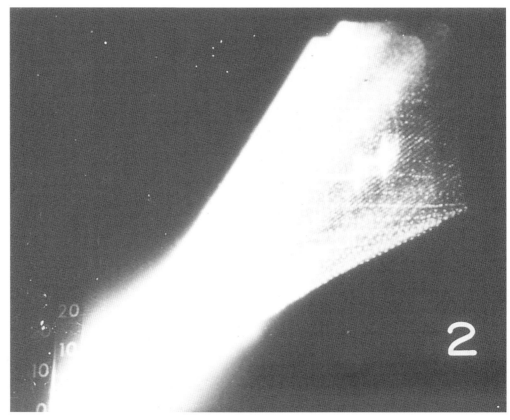

Howard landed in Goose Bay, refueled and departed for London before the F-94 landed, and the pilots had no opportunity to compare notes. The entire crew was, however, "questioned at length by USAF Intelligence at Goose Bay" (who, Howard commented "seemed totally unsurprised at the sighting…there had been several others in the Labrador area recently"). Howard was convinced that the UFO "was controlled intelligently," and later described his experience as "the strangest 80-mile journey of my life."

The Utica Sighting

At about 12:15 PM on June 23, 1955, a Mohawk Airlines DC-3 was cruising at about 3,000 feet about 15 miles east of Utica, New York, when the copilot noticed an object passing approximately 500 feet above at an angle of about 20 degrees from vertical. Moving at "great speed," it was "light gray, almost round, and it had a center line." The sky was overcast at 4,000 feet, but visibility was good below.

It was observed that beneath the center line there were at least four windows which emitted a bright blue-green light. "It was not rotating but went straight." The pilot also saw the UFO, and the two men watched it for several miles. As the distance between the DC-3 and the UFO increased, the lights "seemed to change color slightly, from greenish to bluish or vice versa." The pilot and copilot computed the speed of the UFO at between

Below: *Another of the many sightings over eastern Canada investigated by Project Blue Book, this disc-shaped UFO was photographed over Ontario on September 29, 1967, by the Foreign Technology Division, AFSC.*

U.F.O. EVALUATING THE EVIDENCE

Above: *The BOAC Stratocruiser, the plane involved in the Labrador sighting, affords particularly wide visibility from the flight deck. The UFO was witnessed at close range for 20 minutes by Captain James Howard, his crew and many of the 30 passengers in clear conditions.*

4,500 and 4,800 MPH. A few minutes after it disappeared from sight, two other aircraft, including a Colonial Airlines DC-3, reported that they saw it, and the Albany, New York, control tower also reported seeing an object. As the Mohawk DC-3 approached Albany, the aircrew overheard that Boston radar had also tracked an object along the same flight path, passing Boston and still eastbound.

Inconsistencies in this report, as noted by Air Force investigators, included the absence of a sonic boom, which should be generated by an object traveling at Mach 6 or better in level flight at 3,500 feet. However, sonic booms occur as an object "breaks" the sound barrier, and this may have occurred a long time before the DC-3s observed the object. Also worth noting is that the flight deck of a DC-3 is not a quiet environment, and the aircrew would have been wearing headsets that would muffle outside sounds.

The Lakenheath Incident

Aside from the wave of sightings around Washington, D.C., in 1952, no widely reported UFO incidents of the 1950s were witnessed by more highly qualified and trained observers than those that occurred near RAF Lakenheath, a Royal Air Force base in southeast England, on the night of August 13–14, 1956.

The incident began when a UFO was seen on radar to be "tailing" a Royal Air Force fighter aircraft. The pilot also apparently saw the UFO below him. The weather was fairly clear, and the probability that false radar signals may have been involved was considered small. The Lakenheath controller stated that there was "little or no traffic or targets on scope," which suggests that there was less chance for interference of false signals.

The radar track of the UFO was seen to "disappear" as it and the fighter overflew the radar at RAF Bentwaters, although near RAF Lakenheath it was

apparently continuous and easily tracked. The "tailing" of the RAF fighter, taken alone, seems to indicate a possible ghost image, but this does not agree with the report that the UFO stopped following the fighter as the latter was returning to its base, heading off instead in a different direction.

The radar operators were careful to calculate the speed of the UFO from distances and elapsed times, and the speeds were reported as consistent from run to run, between stationary episodes. This behavior would be somewhat consistent with reflections from moving atmospheric layers, but not in so many different directions. Statements by other observers that meteors were numerous imply that they could accurately distinguish meteors.

Even the most hard-nosed official studies—such as the 1968 Scientific Study of Unidentified Flying Objects (SSUFO)—have concluded that this is one of the "most puzzling and unusual cases" in the radar/visual UFO files. "The apparently rational, intelligent behavior of the UFO suggests a mechanical device of unknown origin as the most probable explanation of this sighting."

During the event, at least one UFO was tracked by air traffic control radar at two U.S. Air Force and Royal Air Force installations. These apparently corresponded to visual sightings of round, white, rapidly moving objects that changed direction abruptly. Interception was attempted by RAF fighter aircraft. One aircraft was vectored to the UFO by ground control radar, and the pilot reported airborne radar contact and radar "gunlock." The UFO appeared to circle around behind the aircraft, and followed it in spite of the pilot's evasive maneuvers. Contact was broken when the aircraft returned to base, low on fuel.

The preponderance of evidence indicates a genuine UFO in this mysterious case. In the winter of 1968, the project

Above: *Pilots of two DC-3 commercial flights observed the sighting of a fast-moving, colored-light UFO near Utica, New York, on June 23, 1955, which was also witnessed by the air control tower in Albany and tracked by radar in Boston as it traveled eastward.*

U.F.O. EVALUATING THE EVIDENCE

Below: *Items recovered from the site of an unexplained incident near RAF Mildenhall, England, in April 1954.*

staff of the SSUFO received an unsolicited letter from one of the principal witnesses, a retired U.S. Air Force noncommissioned officer, who was the Watch Supervisor at the ground control station on the night in question. When copies of the Project Blue Book files on the case were received by SSUFO in August 1968, the accuracy of the account of this witness, as given in the letter, was seen as remarkable. It was apparently written from memory 12 years after the incident. There were a number of minor discrepancies, mostly a matter of figures (the C-47 at 5,000 feet was actually at 4,000 feet), but the major details of the letter were corroborated by the Blue Book account.

The writer was an air traffic controller with 20 years of service, the last 16 years as a radar operator or supervisor. He was the supervisor on duty on the 5:00 PM to midnight shift, and was at the coordinating desk when he received a call from the radar operator asking whether he had any targets on his scope traveling at 4,000 MPH. The radar operator reported that his team had watched a target proceed from a point 30 or 40 miles east to a point 40 miles west of RAF Bentwaters and pass directly over Bentwaters (also a U.S. Air Force station). He said the tower reported seeing it go by as a blurry light. A C-47 transport aircraft flying over the base at 4,000 feet altitude also reported seeing it as a blurred light that passed under his aircraft, but there was no report as to the estimated distance below the aircraft.

The supervisor immediately had all controllers start scanning the radar scopes, each set on a different range, from 10 miles to 200 miles radius of Lakenheath. He had not yet contacted anyone by telephone, as he was skeptical of the report. As they watched, the stationary target started moving at a

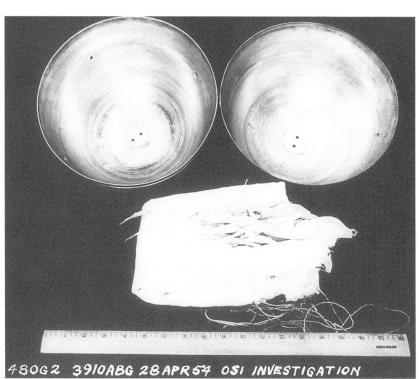

480G2 3910ABG 28APR54 OSI INVESTIGATION

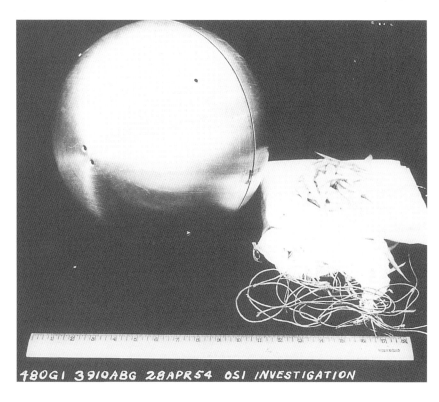

480G1 3910ABG 28APR54 OSI INVESTIGATION

speed of 400 to 600 MPH in a north-by-northeast direction until it reached a point about 20 miles north-northwest of RAF Lakenheath. There was no slow start or build-up to this speed.

The supervisor then called to report all the facts—including the first report from RAF Bentwaters—to the command post and the local commanding officer of the US Air Force Communications Squadron. As he was reporting, the target made several changes in location, always in a straight line, always at about 600 MPH and always from a stationary point with no build-up in speed. Changes in location varied from eight to 20 miles, and it was stationary between movements for three to six minutes.

It was decided to scramble two RAF Venom interceptors to investigate. The interceptor aircraft approached RAF Lakenheath from the southwest. Radio and radar contact was established with the aircraft at a point about 30 miles southwest, inbound to RAF Lakenheath.

The object remained stationary throughout the intercept. Shortly after ground control told the first interceptor pilot he was a half mile from the UFO, he said. "Roger,...I've got my guns locked on him." Then he paused and said, "Where did he go? Do you still have him?" Ground control replied, "Roger, it appeared he got behind you and he's still there." There were now two targets on radar, one behind the other at the same speed and very close, but two separate, distinct targets.

The UFO was so swift in circling behind the interceptor that the pilot had missed it entirely, although it was seen

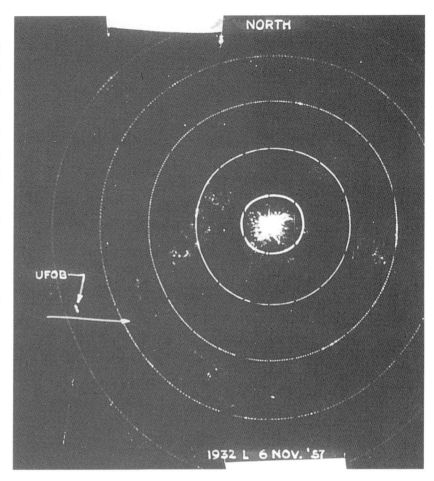

by the controllers. The pilot told ground control he would shake the UFO and try it again. He climbed, dived and circled, but the UFO acted as if it was glued close behind him. The pilot continued trying to shake the UFO for about 10 minutes. Ground control could tell from his occasional comments that he was becoming anxious.

Finally the pilot said, "I'm returning to station. Let me know if he follows me. I'm getting low on petrol." The UFO followed him only a short distance as he headed south-southwest, and then it stopped. Ground control advised the interceptor that the UFO target was now stationary about 10 miles south of RAF Lakenheath. He acknowledged this message, and almost immediately the

Above: *Radar readings have been significant aids to tracking UFO activity in some of the most mysterious cases, from Washington, D.C., to Lakenheath. Such readings, like this one from a Missouri radar station in 1957, provide evidence that investigators can compare with witness testimony during their evaluations.*

Above: *This cluster of UFOs was photographed on March 4, 1962, over Sheffield, Yorkshire, an area of England in which numerous UFO sightings have been reported by credible witnesses since the 1950s.*

second interceptor called on the same frequency. The second interceptor pilot called the first pilot by name, asking, "Did you see anything?" "I saw something," came the reply. "But I'll be damned if I know what it was…. He got behind me and I did everything I could to get behind him and I couldn't. It's the damnedest thing I've ever seen."

Ground control gave the second pilot the location of the UFO and said that they still didn't have him on radar, but expected to shortly. The pilot delayed answering for several seconds, and then reported that he was returning to base because his engine was malfunctioning.

Ground control personnel were instructed by the communications squadron commander to keep watching the target, which finally left radar coverage in a northerly direction, moving at a speed of about 600 MPH.

The air control supervisor made out a written report in detail for the officers in charge of the facility, and was told that unless he was contacted later for further information, the officers would "take care of it."

The maneuvers of this object were extraordinary. The fact that radar and ground visual observations were made on its rapid acceleration and abrupt stops certainly lend credence to the report. It is still widely believed that these sightings were not of any known meteorological or astronomical origin.

In an early Blue Book evaluation, it was suggested that the visual sightings might have been caused by the Perseid meteors. However, as Professor Hynek pointed out: "It seems highly unlikely, for instance, that the Perseid meteors could have been the cause of the sightings, especially in view of the statement of observers that shooting stars were exceptionally numerous that evening, thus implying that they were able to distinguish the two phenomena. Further, if any credence can be given to the maneuvers of the objects as sighted visually and by radar, the meteor hypothesis must be ruled out."

The Lakenheath sighting is of particular significance because, like the 1952 Washington sightings, the UFO was observed both visually and on radar by a large number of highly credible observers, including Royal Air Force and U.S. Air Force pilots, radar operators and air traffic controllers.

From New Guinea to America's Heartland

On May 28, 1965, an egg-shaped silver object was seen by the crew of an Australian Ansett Airlines DC-4 flying from Brisbane to Port Moresby, New Guinea. From approximately 3:25 to 3:40 PM, the UFO followed the aircraft. Captain John Barker, the copilot, commented: "I had always scoffed at these reports, but—I saw it. We all saw it. It was under intelligent control, and it was certainly no known aircraft."

During the early morning hours of August 2, 1965, the Wichita Weather Bureau's airport station was contacted by the dispatcher of the Sedgwick County, Kansas, Sheriff's Department. A UFO had been sighted in the sky near Wellington, Kansas, about 25 miles south of Wichita. Meanwhile, the radar operator, John S. Shockley, observed what appeared to be an aircraft near Udall, Kansas, 15 miles northeast of Wellington. This target moved northward at 40 to 50 MPH. The weather was clear, and the wind light from the southwest.

During the next hour and a half several of these targets were observed on the radar scope over central Kansas, moving slowly northward, and occasionally remaining stationary or moving erratically. Shockley checked with the Wichita Radar Approach Control. However, they were not able to observe a target simultaneously, with the exception of one south of McConnell AFB, near Wichita.

Later, a target was observed about seven miles northwest of Wellington, moving slowly southward. The Wellington Police Department was contacted, and two officers went to investigate. The target passed about one mile west of the city, as observed on radar, but the officers did not observe it visually until it was southwest of the city. They described it as a greenish-blue light that moved slowly away from them.

The dispatcher called again, with a report that two police officers at Caldwell, 35 miles south of Wichita, had sighted an object near the ground east of the city. A target was observed on radar

U.F.O. EVALUATING THE EVIDENCE

Below: *Aerospace expert Stuart Nixon, executive director of the National Investigations Committee on Aerial Phenomena (NICAP), which was founded in Washington, D.C., in 1956 to conduct a civilian study of UFOs. This 1971 photograph was determined by NICAP to be a hoax. The U.S. Air Force derided NICAP as a "hobbyist" group, despite its serious investigative efforts.*

about two miles northwest of the city that moved northward and disappeared.

At daybreak, the dispatcher reported that the Wellington officers had an object in sight east of the city. Radar indicated a target in that area moving southward about 45 MPH. Four or five people stopped their cars and watched the object with the officers. It was described as egg-shaped, made of a highly polished silver metal and about the size of three automobiles.

Shortly after 6:00 AM, a radar target was observed five miles north of Wellington moving southward. The target moved directly over the city, to a point 10 miles south of the city, where it disappeared. The officers in Wellington

were contacted, but were not able to observe this object visually. Due to the swift and concealing actions of the federal government, little attention was drawn to the incident in Wellington.

The Wave of 1966–1968
During 1966, there was an especially large number of UFOs observed by airliner crews around the world. Six objects were seen by the flight crew of an East African Airways DC-3 flying between Mombasa and Nairobi, Kenya. During December 1966, three Finnair crews observed a formation of three cigar-shaped objects accompanied by 10 lighter and darker round objects. This strange grouping was observed flying

U.S. Air Force Procedures: Regulation AFR 200-2

On December 24, 1959, the U.S. Air Force issued a memo to all personnel stating that the Air Force was concerned with the reporting of all UFOs "as a possible threat to the security of the United States and its forces, and secondly, to determine technical aspects involved." The memo was known as AFR 200-2.

Secretary of the Air Force Dudley Sharp gave specific instructions that Air Force personnel were to release "only [UFO] reports...where the object has been definitely identified as a familiar object."

AFR 200-2 read in part: "Unidentified Flying Objects—sometimes treated lightly by the press and referred to as 'flying saucers'—must be rapidly and accurately identified as serious USAF business." The memo identified three criteria of concern:

1. Is the object a threat to the defense of the United States?
2. Does it contribute to technical or scientific knowledge?
3. The U.S. Air Force has a responsibility to explain to the American people through public information media what is going on in their skies.

AFR 200-2 required that every UFO sighting be evaluated and reported to the Air Technical Intelligence Center at Wright-Patterson AFB, and that explanation to the public be "realistic and knowledgeable." It outlined orderly, qualified reporting and public information procedures. At each Air Force base, responsibility for handling UFOs would rest with either intelligence, operations, the Provost Marshal or the Information Officer—in that order of preference. A specific officer would be designated responsible: someone with experience in investigative techniques and also, if possible, scientific or technical background. This officer would have authority to obtain the assistance of specialists on the base, be equipped with binoculars, a camera, a Geiger counter, a magnifying glass and a source for containers in which to store samples.

It was assumed in the Air Force in 1959 that reports of UFO sightings would tend to increase, since the public were now more aware of the phenomena. Public and media interest in manned space flight was also at an unprecedented level at the time—the Mercury astronauts were selected in 1959. Indeed, there was more positive interest in space travel during the few years following 1959 than at any other time, with the exception of the period in 1969 that followed the first Moon landing.

Above: *A 1965 photograph with a one-minute exposure showing two objects that remained stationary over Buenos Aires, Argentina, for 10 minutes before departing at very high speed.*

separation with time. At the greatest angular separation, the lights appeared to one of the observers to be connected by a body with windows. Objects protruding from the main body were also reported. The UFO appeared to fly "in formation" with the aircraft for about two minutes, and then was lost to view behind the wings of the aircraft.

The witnesses described two very bright lights, one of which was pulsating; from the two lights came two thin beams of light (like aircraft landing lights), which moved from a V-shape to an inverted "V." At one point the object seemed to emit a shower of sparks, similar to fireworks. There appeared to be a solid shape between the two white lights, which was thicker in the middle and tapered outward. There was also a strip of low light between the white lights that was yellowish in color, much like cabin lights of an aircraft.

It was suggested that the sighting may have been the result of the re-entry of fragments of the Agena rocket booster that had been used to launch the unmanned Gemini 2 spacecraft in January 1965. However, the account did not describe an Agena, and the re-entry of the Agena fragments occurred 33 minutes before the UFO sighting, and 250 miles away.

The apparent "pacing" of the aircraft by the object for an estimated two minutes is a puzzling feature of the sighting, but it is consistent with many other UFO sightings of that era. The rapid deceleration of a re-entering fragment of space debris—such as the Agena—might have given the impression to the

over Hamburg, Germany, and over Maarianhamina, Finland, at least 900 miles away. Another Finnair Caravelle jetliner spotted the formation near Helsinki-Oulu, Finland, 250 miles from Maarianhamina.

Among the more curious of several Latin American sightings was one that occurred during the winter of 1966. Four members of the crew of a DC-8 on a night flight from Lima, Peru, to Mexico City reported sighting two bright lights that appeared to increase their angular

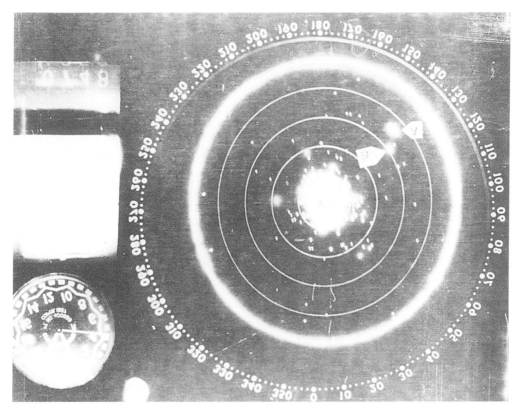

Left: *Radar readings capture the presence of UFOs over the Atlantic Ocean during November 1964.*

Below: *Mysterious lights over Naha, Okinawa, Japan, on October 7, 1962.*

crew that the object was pacing the aircraft, since it could have appeared close to 90 degrees on the left side of the aircraft for some minutes during its final descent into the atmosphere. However, the captain's description suggests the intriguing possibility of an intelligently guided vehicle, which, in his words, "is a craft with speed and maneuverability unknown to us." This captain had some 26 years of flying experience.

On May 4, 1966, near Charleston, West Virginia, the pilot of a Braniff Airlines Boeing 707, flying at 33,000 feet, observed on his left side what appeared to be a fast-flying aircraft with landing lights. The 707's airborne radar also recorded this object. The weather was generally clear, but there were severe thunderstorms in the area. The pilot requested that the radar operator at Indianapolis ARTC look for traffic nearby, and the radar picked up a track, which made a sweeping turn and disappeared off the scope to the southwest.

An American Airlines pilot flying 20 miles behind the Braniff plane saw the object as well. It appeared to him to be a normal aircraft with landing lights. This pilot stated he had often seen U.S. Air Force aircraft with lights during aerial refueling missions. The American pilot estimated the speed of the UFO to be between 750 and 800 MPH. No unusual maneuvers were performed, or any that were beyond known military aircraft capabilities at the time. Though no known aircraft was in the area, the official Air Force explanation is that the unknown craft was simply an aircraft with landing lights on.

Early in 1967, another nocturnal light reported by a pilot attracted interest from investigators. On February 2, Captain Oswaldo Sanviti was flying a Faucett Airlines DC-4 at 7,000 feet between Chiclayo and Lima, Peru, when he saw a "very luminous object....It had so much light that all the passengers of our plane saw and started to be very nervous and exclaimed, 'There is an *OVNI*' [Spanish for UFO]. After a while the *OVNI* passed over my plane and stopped right over us. At this moment we noticed a 15 degree left oscillation on our radio compass....All the lights in the main cabin started to reduce intensity...[the object] moved over,...increasing its light about 50 percent into a bluish light, and disappeared with a fantastic speed. After five minutes, the *OVNI* returned with another one and situated itself a close distance [from] our tail section. We flew in this formation [for]

five minutes before landing at the Lima International Airport."

A very similar event occurred in Europe about six weeks later, on March 22, when a British European Airways Vickers Vanguard was flying over the Bay of Biscay in Spain. It was a clear night, and crew members spotted what seemed to be a bright star. After a few minutes, it started toward them. As it moved, it changed color from bright white to red, blue and green. They also reported that it executed inexplicable, high-speed aerobatics. It was then joined by a similar object. The Vanguard crew contacted nearby Bordeaux, France, radar control, and were told that there was unidentified traffic where the objects were being observed. It is rumored that the first officer, Graham Sheppard, was told by the captain, a World War II veteran, not to tell anyone about the event because it could damage his credibility as a pilot.

If 1966 and 1967 had been particularly rich in commercial pilot sightings, then 1968 saw a number of intriguing general aviation sightings. There were several significant sightings in the Puget Sound area, Washington. At about 10:00 PM on July 7, Rudy Malaspina was flying a single engine Piper Cherokee aircraft from Roach Harbor in the San Juan Islands to Boeing Field in Seattle, when he was passed by a formation of bright lights that separated abruptly over Seattle's Queen Anne Hill. On October 30, near Vancouver, British Columbia, a formation of four lights in the sky was observed to circle one another, and then split and move in opposite directions.

Three weeks later, on August 22, 1968, two pilots in a Piper Navajo flying at 8,000 feet at 195 knots between Adelaide and Perth, Australia, observed a group of what they thought to be aircraft pacing the Navajo. There was a large object in the middle of four or five smaller objects. After the pilots had watched these UFOs for about 10 minutes, the UFOs split up and flew away.

An intriguing radar-visual event occurred at 5:40 PM on November 26, 1968. Controllers in the Bismarck, North Dakota, and Great Falls, Montana, control towers simultaneously tracked a pair of UFOs by radar, and three Bismarck controllers observed two brightly illuminated objects.

The Invisible UFO

In many UFO incidents, radar targets are found to agree with visual reports. In some cases, visual sightings are unconfirmed by radar observers, but the Colorado Springs incident is unusual in that it is a "radar-only" case, where the UFO could not be seen visually, even by trained observers. On May 13, 1967, Colorado Springs Airport was reporting visibility of 15 miles, with overcast conditions, scattered showers and snow showers in the area. It should be noted that Colorado Springs Airport is not "horizon-limited," and visibility of 100 miles is routinely reported on clear days.

At about 4:40 PM, a UFO was first picked up on radar as a Braniff Airlines flight touched down on runway 35. The UFO track behaved like a ghost echo, perhaps a ground return being reflected from the aircraft. The UFO blip appeared

at about twice the range of the Braniff blip, and on the same azimuth, although the elevation angle appeared to have been different.

When the Braniff airliner touched down, however, the UFO blip pulled to the right (east) and passed over the airport at an indicated height of about 200 feet. As pointed out by the Federal Aviation Administration (FAA), this is precisely the correct procedure for an overtaking aircraft, or one testing an approach but not intending to touch down.

Although the UFO track passed within 1.5 miles of the control tower, and the

Below: *On June 21, 1968, this disc-shaped object was photographed over Flushing, New York City.*

Blue Book Gallery II

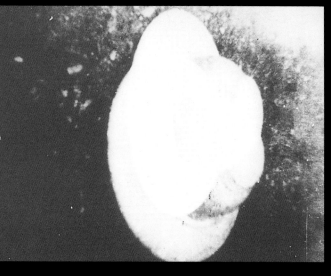

A selection of UFO sightings in the United States from the Blue Book files of the 1967 wave: opposite, above: October 22, a low-flying object in Milledgeville, Georgia; opposite, below: January 25, a disc-shaped object in Hampton, Virginia; Left: a series of photographs taken of a large, unusual UFO on June 1, in North San Juan, California; and below: a low-flying, disc-shaped UFO photographed over a home in Lexington, Missouri.

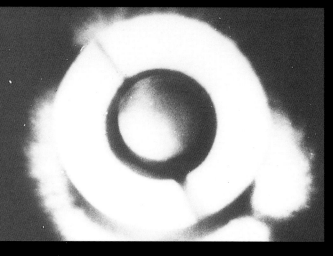

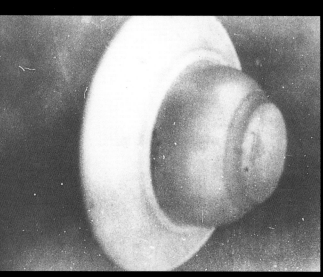

Above: *Ramey Air Force Base photographed this large, white spherical object over Puerto Rico on April 16, 1967.*

personnel there were alerted to the situation, the UFO was not visible, even through binoculars. A Continental Airlines flight, which was monitored three to four miles behind the UFO at first contact, was flying in the same direction, but did not see it either.

Both the radar transmitting antennas at Colorado Springs were located to the east of runway 35, about 1,000 feet apart. A ghost echo was ruled out because it will not normally be indicated at a height of 200 feet while the ghost-producer is on the ground, as was the case here. If an indirect ghost were involved, the ghost echo would have always appeared well to the east of the Braniff jetliner, not at the same azimuth. The radar flight characteristics of the UFO in this case were all compatible with the hypothesis that the unknown was a century-series jet fighter—such as an F-100, F-104 or F-106—yet nothing was seen or heard.

The Vandenberg AFB Sighting

The most compelling UFO sightings are those in which multiple trained witnesses observe UFOs over a period of time, as was the case over Washington in 1952 and RAF Lakenheath in 1956. A somewhat similar radar-visual sighting occurred on October 6, 1967, near Vandenberg AFB, California. The events began at about 8:00 PM with a visual sighting of an object with colored lights that hovered over the Pacific Ocean. Missile-tracking radar at Vandenberg picked up many unidentified targets—most of them moving—and tracked them. Most of the moving targets permitted radar lock-on. They moved at speeds up to 80 knots, and sometimes returned very strong echoes.

The Vandenberg AFB sightings were exceptional because of the high professional qualifications of the observers. Two were officials of the Western Missile Test Range, each with 17 years of experience as a naval aviator. One official had 10,000 hours as an air intercept and final approach controller. The other had also been an air intercept controller. A third, who was the range air control officer on the night of the first sighting, had 11 years of experience with ground and airborne electronics systems. Six others were radar operators employed by private contractors on the base, all of whom had extensive experience. They displayed what investigators later described as "impressive understanding of the sophisticated radar systems they were operating and good comprehension of radar engineering principles." The radar systems involved in the sightings included an FPS-16 C-band tracking radar with 1.2 degree beam; a TPQ-18 C-band tracking radar, 0.4 degree beam; an M33 X-band tracking radar, an ARCER L-band search radar; and a GERTS X-band tracking and command radar.

While most objects were sighted over the ocean, some targets appeared over land, to the east and north toward Santa Maria and Arroyo Grande. The radar targets were still being observed when the equipment was closed down at about 2:30 AM, yet no aircraft were known to be in the area, and three flights of fighter aircraft sent out to investigate found nothing unusual.

Project Blue Book notified the Scientific Study of Unidentified Flying Objects (SSUFO) of this sighting shortly afterward. It was also reported that, in a test three nights later, it had been established that radar at the base again observed "bogies" similar to those on the night of the original sighting. SSUFO Project investigators and others visited the site twice.

The witnesses told SSUFO that for about 30 minutes, from 8:00 PM on October 6, a missile range official observed an object visually from his home. He called another official, also at home three miles to the south, who confirmed the sighting at an altitude of 10 to 15 degrees. The second observer reported that the object, as seen through 7 x 50 binoculars, appeared the size of a large thumbtack, elliptical in shape and having a red and green light separated by a distance about the "wingspan of an aircraft." The object appeared stationary and fuzzy, like a spinning top.

At 8:45, the range control officer confirmed the observation. To him it appeared to have constant white, red and green or blue colors. They "looked like the running lights on a stationary object." He gave its bearing as 290 degrees, range several miles, and he estimated its altitude at approximately 10,000 feet. He suggested that the object looked like a helicopter.

At about the same time, the FPS-16 radar, in search mode, locked onto two strong targets, one moving and one stationary. The stationary target appeared in the general direction of the visual sighting. The original interpretation was that it was, in fact, a helicopter.

At 9:00 PM, the range control officer checked for possible air traffic in the Vandenberg AFB area with several other air bases. All reported that they had no aircraft in flight in the area. Using its FPS-16 in lock-on automatic mode, another base reported strong targets headed toward Vandenberg AFB. Because of the narrow beam of the radar the targets were presumed to be in line. The TPQ-18 radar at Vandenberg AFB was brought into operation, and saw many targets. One, at eight miles range and 4,000 feet altitude, proceeded south at low speed. Another strong target approached and went directly overhead, producing an extremely strong, 80 decibel signal. Three people went outside the radar shack, but were unable to see any object. At one time, the TPQ-18 saw four targets.

One of the strongest targets on the TPQ-18 radar appeared to separate into eight objects, after which it was necessary to switch to manual to separate the signals. North American Air Defense Command (NORAD) surveillance radar at Vandenberg AFB operated at a frequency quite different from the tracking radar, and it saw no targets, but its operator reported clutter or "possible jamming."

One visual appeared to move toward the observers so alarmingly that one of them yelled, "Duck!" Another object, dull in color but showing red, white and green lighting, moved south out of visual range. Another, resembling a bright fireball, moved on a zigzag course from north to south. Two radar operators reported, "The radar didn't get locked onto what we saw. By the time the radar slaved to us, the object was gone visually, and the radar didn't see anything....It looked like a fireball coming down through there. Like a helicopter coming down the coast, at low elevation. We got the 13-power telescope on it." Then it grew smaller and smaller until it disappeared.

Below: *This UFO, photographed over Torrance, was one of many sightings reported in California, in 1967.*

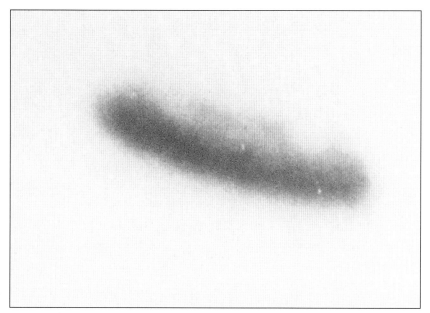

At 11:10 PM, Air Defense Command (ADC) scrambled the first of three flights of interceptor aircraft to investigate the situation. The tape of the conversations with the radar sites and other bases evidenced considerable confusion. The fighters were handed off to Vandenberg AFB Range Control by the FAA and controlled locally. Range Control tried to vector the fighters, but found it impossible to do so systematically. By the time the second flight came in, the controllers were so busy with the aircraft that they no longer observed any unidentified targets. They did observe a moderate amount of clutter in the west and southwest quadrants. None of the fighter pilots saw anything visually, though one pilot observed something repeatedly on his infrared detector, at a distance. Another aircraft did lock onto a target, but it was then found to be a ship.

The weather officer reported that there was an inversion layer at 1,800 to 2,200 feet, but the unidentified targets were reported to be higher. An unusually strong temperature inversion provided favorable conditions for both visual and radar mirage effects. It was suggested that mirages of ships below the normal horizon might account for the stationary or slow objects. The higher, faster radar targets were theorized to have been birds! In a weather sequence that moved a trough line and a low pressure center southeastward on the day prior to the sighting, a dome of high pressure formed over the Great Basin and a surge of warm air moved in. Weather stations near the coast all showed abnormally warm temperatures at a time of day when a sea breeze would ordinarily have provided a cooling influence. This effect led Air Force investigators to conclude that all of the UFO sightings—both visual and on radar—were mirages. The SSUFO team accepted that conclusion and the case was officially closed.

The Alamogordo "Specks"

No region of the world is known to have experienced a higher concentration of UFO sightings by military and other qualified personnel over a longer time span than south-central New Mexico, specifically the area around the U.S. Army's White Sands Missile Range (an area which includes, of course, Roswell). While tests at White Sands might lead average citizens to report "strange things in the sky," many important sightings have been reported by knowledgeable personnel stationed there and at nearby installations.

One of the most important UFO incidents of the decade occurred in the winter of 1967; it was evaluated by J. Allen Hynek when he was a consultant for the Scientific Study of Unidentified Flying Objects (SSUFO). Daylight visual sightings of "silvery specks" overhead were reported, but pilots of investigating aircraft saw nothing. Two radar sites—White Sands Mission Control and Elephant Mountain Radar—concurrently detected several intermittent stationary targets at the location, and then a single target that moved slowly for several minutes. It then disappeared on one radar, while on the other it described an approximately circular course at high speed.

After hovering near Ruidoso for about an hour, the UFOs moved in a nearly circular, clockwise flight path that had its center roughly at White Sands Mission Control, near Alamogordo. This near-complete circle, with a radius of roughly 30 miles, was completed by the UFOs in about 12 minutes.

Hynek and his team examined the radar plots and interviewed the Holloman AFB public information officer and the radar operators. They discovered that at 10:25 AM, a young man had telephoned the base UFO officer from the mountains near Ruidoso to report "silvery specks" passing overhead. During about 30 minutes, he had seen two or three groups of 30 to 40 such objects moving southwest. The public affairs officer finished his conversation with the witness at 10:50 AM and requested that two aircraft be sent to the reported location. They found nothing unusual.

Above: *On July 7, 1967, another mysterious object was photographed in California—this time over San Luis Obispo.*

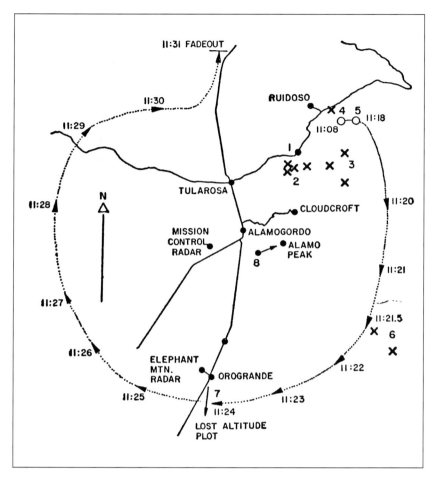

Above: *The investigators' map of the circular course of the puzzling, multiple-witness Alamagordo sighting.*

The public affairs officer also asked range surveillance radar at White Sands at Elephant Mountain to seek the objects. About 10:55 AM both plotted four objects about five miles south of the visual sighting, and a little later three more objects. All were stationary, but intermittent, so that the radar tracking equipment could not "lock on" to them.

Then at 11:08 AM, both radar plotted a slow-moving object at 25,000 feet altitude, and tracked it for 10 minutes while it moved three or four miles eastward. At 11:18 AM, it disappeared from the Elephant Mountain radar screen, while the radar at Mission Control showed it moving southward at Mach 1.2. It continued on its approximately circular course.

At 11:21 AM, both radar showed two stationary but intermittent objects 35 miles southeast of Holloman AFB. Mission Control radar continued to follow the fast-moving target on its circular course until it abruptly climbed to 80,000 feet above Orogrande, and followed it on around to the north, until it appeared to go out of range due north of Mission Control at 100,000 feet altitude, at 11:31 AM.

During the tracking of the circular course, the operator stated that he thought the radar was malfunctioning. The following day, the radar supervisor reported that evaluation of the Mission Control radar record indicated that the instrument had plotted a noise track. The subsequent evaluation by the civilian radar supervisory staff reached the same conclusion, though no explanation was advanced for the object's disappearance from both radar screens at once.

Rumor or Cover-Up?
Throughout the history of UFO sightings and evaluations, there are cases in which official spokespersons simply deny that a sighting took place. In evaluating the evidence in such a case, one must be aware of the strong possibility that such denials are true, and that rumors of official sightings are, in fact, just that—unfounded rumors. On the other hand, experience has shown that "official sources" have at times issued false denials for various reasons. False denials often lead to elaborate cover-ups that are constructed in order to protect the accountability of the original denial.

Since the Watergate era of the early 1970s, the American public has been less willing to give government reports the benefit of the doubt. A decade earlier, however, there was a greater willingness to accept official statements. By the early 1960s, this was especially true with UFO reports because the plethora of reports that lacked credible evidence had led most people to regard witnesses as—in the vernacular of the time—"kooks." Against this backdrop, many serious observers were reluctant to report sightings. This was certainly true of test pilots and people involved in leading-edge aeronautical experiments: to be branded a "kook" could hamper one's career.

By the mid–1960s, there were few aeronautical experiments more leading-edge than those involving the North American Aviation X-15. The X-15 flew higher (354,200 feet) and faster (4,534 MPH) under its own power than any other airplane before or since, making it a milestone in the history of technology.

Thus, it should come as little surprise that the incident of UFOs in pursuit of an X-15 was first made known to the Scientific Study of Unidentified Flying Objects (SSUFO) through a rumor. This rumor was relayed to SSUFO in 1967 by "a source considered to be reliable"—a civilian who had previously worked at Edwards AFB, California, where the X-15 program was managed jointly by the Air Force and NASA. This man, whose name SSUFO did not disclose, reported that six UFOs had followed an X-15 flight and that motion pictures of the event should be available from the Air Force.

While the SSUFO report declined to give the date on which the X-15 incident occurred, researcher and former NASA staffer Richard Haines has noted that it is rumored to have happened on April 30, 1962. On that date, NASA test pilot Joseph A. Walker flew an X-15 (tail number 6-6670) to 246,700 feet, the highest altitude yet achieved in the X-15 program. The X-15's rear-viewing camera captured five disc-shaped or cylindrical objects flying in echelon formation. X-15 program records indicate that ice, which accumulated on the tail at very high altitude, was observed breaking off during the flight.

Before initiating a field investigation, SSUFO project members checked with base operations at Edwards AFB for confirmation of the rumor. One would have expected that SSUFO would have been told about the film of the ice breaking off the X-15 tail. However, SSUFO was told that there was no log book record of a UFO report and no X-15 flight on the day in question.

SSUFO reported that the rumor persisted, "with indications that official secrecy was associated with the event." A responsible base employee, who wished to remain anonymous, had reassured SSUFO's source that there was a sighting by pilots and control tower operators. The employee had left the base for temporary duty elsewhere, and his replacement was unable to obtain details of the event, but was quoted as saying that there was apparently something to it because "they are not just flatly denying it."

The base employee was contacted at his temporary assignment by an SSUFO

U.F.O. EVALUATING THE EVIDENCE

Right: This low-flying disclike object with a fin or tail was photographed over Mount Clemens, Michigan, in January 1967, a year during which advanced aeronautical experiments, as well as UFO sightings, were commonplace in the United States.

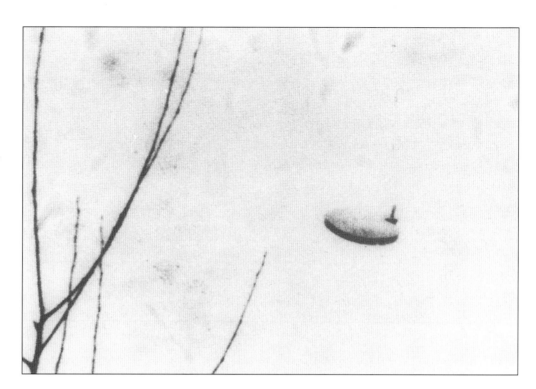

project investigator. He said he did not know much about the incident, since all the information had been turned over to the public information officer, who was the only one at the base at liberty to discuss it. He had been told by the director of information to "stay out of that."

Attempts to learn more from the public information officer were met with apparent evasion. The director was unavailable for comment. A request was then made through the Pentagon for determination of whether or not a UFO event had, in fact, been reported by the base on the day specified. A Pentagon officer transmitted a request for clarification to the base director of information, which was answered by an assistant who denied the rumor.

While it is true that this report was never more than a rumor, SSUFO reported that "It is also true that project investigators were not able satisfactorily to confirm or deny that a UFO incident

had occurred. Attempts to evaluate the rumor were met with evasion and uncooperative responses to our inquiries by base information."

Astronaut Sightings

Consistent with the hypothesis that UFOs are of extraterrestrial origin, one would presume that UFOs are also observed by astronauts traveling in space. Certainly, such occurrences are common in science fiction films and novels. However, the literature on UFO sightings in outer space is sparse.

A few reports of such sightings emerged from the former Soviet Union's space programs, although a 1990 sighting by G.M. Manakov from space station *Mir* was the first to receive widespread publicity.

In the case of the U.S. space program, there was a concentration of UFO reports during the Gemini program of 1965–66, and another widely reported event happened during Space Shuttle mission STS-48 in September 1991. Both of these happened to coincide with a major wave of UFO interest.

One case that involved astronauts occurred on November 12, 1969, shortly after the end of Project Blue Book. The astronauts of Apollo 12—Alan Bean, Pete Conrad and Dick Gordon—observed what appeared to them to be a flashing light following them on a course to the moon. This observation was confirmed by ground-based astronomical observatories in Europe. There are also rumors of suppressed reports of UFO sightings by Apollo astronauts on the Moon.

There have been no official reports of UFOs by U.S. astronauts since the 1960s. This is partially a result of official NASA policy, in which the space agency wishes to distance itself from the UFO enthusiasts with skepticism.

During the Gemini program, however, UFOs were still considered "serious business," and were regarded with a more open mind. While many sightings are written off as space boosters or space "junk," three visual sightings were reported by the Gemini astronauts while in orbit; they remain unexplained. Two occurred during Gemini 4 and one during Gemini 7.

On June 4, 1965, as Gemini 4 was in free drifting flight somewhere over the Pacific Ocean, astronaut James McDivitt observed a cylindrical object that appeared to have arms sticking out, a description suggesting a spacecraft with an antenna, or the second stage of a Titan booster rocket. He was quite famil-

iar with such objects and was certain that it was neither. It had a white or silvery appearance in daylight.

The conditions under which astronauts made their observations are similar to those in the front seat of a small car with no side or rear windows and a partially covered, smudged windshield. The windows permitted only a limited forward view and were never entirely clean: the difficulties imposed by the scattering of light from deposits on the window were severe. Attempts were made to eliminate the smudging by means of temporary covers jettisoned once orbit was achieved, but even then deposits collected on the inside of the outer pane of glass. The net result was that scattered light hampered the astronauts' observations.

As McDivitt photographed the object, he formed the impression that the object was nearby and closing in. He felt that evasive action might be necessary. The object was lost to view when the sun shone on the window. He tried unsuccessfully to get it back into view.

When the astronauts landed, the photographic film was given to NASA, whose photo interpreter released three or four pictures, but McDivitt said that these were definitely not of the object he had seen. His personal inspection of the film later revealed what he had seen, although the quality of the image was poor. McDivitt believed that the object was probably an unmanned satellite, possibly one of the Corona series of reconnaissance spacecraft that would remain classified until 1995.

The North American Air Defense Command (NORAD) made an investigation of possible satellites at the time, and suggested that the object might have been a Pegasus micro-meteorite observer satellite, which was 1,200 miles away at the time. This is improbable. When fully extended, Pegasus B had a maximum dimension of about 100 feet, so at 1,200 miles, it would have been much too small for the structure of the craft to be resolved, and thus does not correspond with the description of "arms sticking out." Another 10 pieces of debris were noted by NORAD, but were of the same size or smaller than Pegasus B.

UFOs are frequently explained as weather phenomena, manmade objects, stars or planets. There is no weather in space, and the objects described were not stars or planets. If they were manmade, the only other possibility is rocket boosters or debris. The rocket booster often achieves orbit along with the pri-

mary spacecraft, and can be seen by the astronauts until the relative orbits have diverged to put the booster out of sight.

Also during Gemini 4, McDivitt observed another UFO, a moving bright light, higher than the spacecraft. He reported that he "saw a satellite, very high…spotted away just like a star on the ground when you see one go by, a long, long ways away. When I saw this satellite go by we were pointed just about directly overhead. It looked like it was going from left to right…back toward the west, so it must have been going from south to north."

While McDivitt referred to this sighting as a satellite, it was higher than Gemini 4 and moving in a polar orbit. It was reported as looking like a "star," so there was no indication of an angular extension or shape.

The suggestion at the time of sighting that this was a satellite was not confirmed

Right: A Gemini spacecraft orbiting the Earth. During the 1965–66 Gemini program, there was a concentration of UFO sightings reported by astronauts.

Left: This NASA photograph shows a cometlike object photographed during the Gemini 4 flight, during which astronauts reported sighting a number of unexplained phenomena.

by a definite identification of a known satellite, but in retrospect, Corona spacecraft were commonly launched into polar orbit, and their existence would not be revealed for another 30 years.

During the flight of Gemini 7, between December 4 and 18, 1965, astronauts Frank Borman and Jim Lovell reported a "bogey at 10 o'clock high." They also had their Titan rocket booster in sight, so they could not mistake it for the object. Borman and Lovell also observed "hundreds of little particles banked on the left out about 3 to 7 miles…I have the booster on my side. It's a brilliant body in the sun, against a black background with trillions of particles on it."

It was suggested that the "bogey" and particles were debris fragments from the launching of Gemini 7, but this is impossible if the objects were traveling in a polar orbit, as it appeared.

Launched on September 12, 1991, STS-48 was the 43rd mission of the Space Shuttle program, and the 13th flight of the Orbiter *Discovery*. It would last 5 days, 8

hours, 27 minutes and 38 seconds, covering a distance of 2,193,670 miles. The primary payload was the Upper Atmosphere Research Satellite, a 14,500-pound observatory spacecraft that would orbit for 18 months. The crew included John O. Creighton, the mission commander, and pilot Kenneth S. Reightler, as well as mission specialists James F. Buchli, Charles D. Gernar and Mark N. Brown.

During the mission, a video camera captured what appeared to be an object or objects flying at high speed above the surface of the Earth and into space. The official NASA interpretation was that the objects were not distant vehicles, but ice particles seen at close range. Possible sources for ice particles might have included propellant—such as nitrogen tetroxide or hydrazine—from the spacecraft's maneuvering system, water from the "dump line" or water from the fuel cell purge lines. Nevertheless, the story of the "STS-48 UFOs" continued to be studied for several years, as the ice theory was not convincing.

7: Review and Termination of Project Blue Book

> "I feel that the Air Force has not been giving out all the available information on the Unidentified Flying Objects. You cannot disregard so many unimpeachable sources."
>
> —John W. McCormack
> Speaker of the House of Representatives, January 1965

By 1966, it had been over 13 years since the U.S. government, at the end of Truman's presidency, had reacted to the series sightings over Washington by setting up the Scientific Advisory Panel on UFOs to study the phenomena. In 1966, Lyndon Johnson was in the middle of his first—and only—elected term of office. There was no dash to tie up loose ends before a new administration took over. But Blue Book and its predecessor agencies had been gathering data for nearly two decades and nothing significant had been concluded.

Another Scientific Board

In a memorandum dated September 28, 1965, Air Force major general E.B. LeBailly, head of the Secretary of the Air Force Office of Information (SAFOI), requested that the military director of the U.S. Air Force Scientific Advisory Board (SAB) organize a "working scientific panel composed of both physical and social scientists" to review Project Blue Book, then operating since March 1952.

In February 1966, the SAB Ad Hoc Committee met to review Project Blue Book's resources, methods and findings.

The committee included the eminent Dr. Carl Sagan, the late Cornell University astronomer who, until his death in 1997, would be one of the most vocal advocates of a search for extraterrestrial intelligence. As with the 1953 panel, the SAB members' scientific credentials were beyond reproach.

To bring themselves up to date, the committee members first reviewed the findings of previous scientific panels on what they called "the UFO problem." The committee heard briefings from the Air Force Systems Command (AFSC), Foreign Technology Division (FTD), which was then collating information on UFO sightings and monitoring evaluations. The FTD, like its predecessor ATIC, was headquartered at Wright-Patterson Air Force Base near Dayton, Ohio.

The committee found Project Blue Book to have been "well organized," even with limited resources—only one officer, a sergeant and a secretary. In 19 years,

Opposite: The microfilms of Project Blue Book photographs contain mysteries that cannot be investigated without the original files. Something in the center portion of this image, taken in Brookesville, Florida, in March 1965, appears to have been censored by Blue Book staff.

10,147 sightings had been recorded and classified. No verified and fully satisfactory evidence had been found of any case that was "outside the framework of presently known science and technology."

However, as the committee looked into selected case histories of UFO sightings, it found that 6 percent (646) of all sightings in the years 1952–65 were listed by the Air Force as "unidentified." Most of these were described as "simply those in which the information available does not provide an adequate basis for analysis."

The Air Force also admitted, "Some of the case records which the Committee looked at that were listed as 'identified' were sightings where the evidence collected was too meager or too indefinite to permit positive listing in the identified category." With a staff of three, this is easy to imagine.

It was also pointed out to the committee that no unidentified objects except those of an astronomical nature had been observed during routine astronomical studies, in spite of the large number of observing hours devoted to the sky. For example, the Palomar Observatory Sky Atlas contains some 5,000 plates made with large instruments with wide fields of view. Of course, most astronomical photographs are long time exposures done at night and would capture fast-moving objects only if they contained a light source.

Because of its mandate to protect American air space, a major concern of the Air Force was whether UFOs represented a danger to the nation. The committee concluded that in the 19 years since the first UFO was sighted, there had been no evidence that unidentified flying objects were a threat to United States national security. Attention then turned to consideration of how the Air Force should handle the scientific aspects of the UFO incidents. Unavoidably, these were related to Air Force public relations—a subject outside the committee's expertise.

The committee responded to the skeleton staff of Project Blue Book by recommending contracts with a few selected universities for scientific teams to evaluate selected UFO sightings promptly and in depth. Each team should include at least one psychologist, preferably in the clinical sphere, and one physical scientist, preferably an astronomer or geophysicist. The universities chosen should be within convenient distance of an Air Force Systems Command base. The Air Force agreed to augment Blue Book staffing by suggesting that at each AFSC base, a local officer skilled in investigation could be designated to work with the university team.

The committee estimated that 100 sightings a year would require close evaluation, at an average of ten man days per sighting. Such a program might bring to light new facts of scientific value. It also decided that Project Blue Book reports should be widely circulated among prominent members of Congress and other public figures to aid public understanding of the USAF's scientific approach to UFOs.

In August 1966, the Air Force contracted with the University of Colorado to undertake evaluations of UFO sightings: little else was done to implement the grandiose ideas of the SAB committee. The Air Force was rapidly losing its official interest in UFOs. Three years later, Project Blue Book would be closed.

The Colorado Project

The decision to establish the Scientific Study of Unidentified Flying Objects (SSUFO) was one of the few recommendations that the U.S. Air Force took from the SAB report. When the Air Force approached the University of Colorado about undertaking the project, a second meeting was held on August 10 to outline the scope of the proposed evaluation. Officers Dr. J. Thomas Ratchford and Dr. William Price, executive director of the Office of Scientific Research (AFOSR), generated enthusiasm, and the university decided to undertake the project under Contract F44620-67-C-0035. Thus, the SSUFO is sometimes referred to as the Colorado Project. Since Dr. Edward U. Condon was asked to head the SSUFO, it is also referred to as the Condon Study.

The contract provided that planning, direction and conclusions of the Colorado Project would be conducted independently of the Air Force. To avoid duplication of effort, the Air Force was ordered to furnish the project with the records of its own earlier work, and to provide support personnel from its bases as requested by Colorado field teams.

The staff assigned to the project was assured that the government would withhold no information on the subject, and that all pertinent facts could be included in the report. However, where UFO sightings involved classified missile launchings or the use of classified radar systems,

this fact would simply be stated: to do more would involve violation of security on military subjects. The first research contract granted $313,000—a sizable sum for the time—to pay for the first 15 months, from November 1966 through January 1968.

The scientific approach to the UFO phenomenon was seen as requiring the services of scientists in such fields as physics, chemistry, aerodynamics and meteorology. Because the primary material consisted mostly of reports from individual observers, the psychology of perception, the physiology of defects of vision and the evaluation of mental states were also involved. Social psychology and social psychiatry could apply in understanding group motivations, which can induce belief in extraordinary hypotheses on the basis of little or no evidence. However, medical and social psychology were distinctly outside the field of expertise of the Colorado staff, which concentrated chiefly on the evaluation of the UFOs themselves.

No less a figure than Dr. J. Allen Hynek—the soon-to-be outspoken skeptic of official explanations—who had served as astronomical consultant to Blue Book, would be available to the SSUFO. The Colorado Project consulted with the National Investigations Committee for Aerial Phenomena (NICAP), one of the organizations that Project Blue Book derided as a "hobbyist" group. The staff also spoke with investigators and scientists from a number of other organizations and universitites. They studied a variety of topics, including the "effects of optical mirages" and "analogous anom-

U.F.O. EVALUATING THE EVIDENCE

Right: Dr. J. Allen Hynek, an astronomer with unimpeachable credentials, became well known for his dedication to the cause of rigorous, scientific research into UFO phenomena.

alies of radio wave propagation as they affect radar," plus reports of disturbances to automobile ignitions and headlights from UFOs.

Though reports by trained observers are common throughout the literature, the SSUFO claimed that its field investigators had difficulty finding reliable observers, and they decried the almost universal lack of physical evidence. In an ideal situation, field teams would not only get their own photographs, but even obtain spectrograms of the light of the UFO, and would make radioactive, magnetic, and sound measurements in its presence. However, they knew this would be virtually impossible. Nearly all UFO sightings are of very short duration, seldom lasting as long as an hour, and usually only a few minutes. In a few cases, some physical evidence has been gathered by investigators at the site where a UFO reportedly landed. As for official U.S. efforts , "In no case did we obtain any convincing evidence of this kind, although every effort was made to do so."

On the subject of UFO field studies, Hynek was reported as having recom-

mended what he called the "FBI treatment" for every report, including thorough interviews of the person(s) who made it and a search in the neighborhood of the sighting for additional witnesses.

When the SSUFO was concluded, Edward Condon wrote that, although it had attempted "to learn from UFO reports anything that could be considered as adding to scientific knowledge, our general conclusion is that nothing has come from the evaluation of UFOs in the past 21 years that has added to scientific knowledge." He added that "further extensive study of UFOs probably cannot be justified in the expectation that science will be advanced thereby."

The SSUFO evaluation focused almost entirely on the physical sciences. In addressing the question as to what, if anything, the federal government should do about UFO reports from the general public, Condon quipped, "We are inclined to think that nothing should be done with them in the expectation that they are going to contribute to the advance of science."

Termination of Project Blue Book
In 1965, General LeBailly had requested that a "working scientific panel composed of both physical and social scientists" review Project Blue Book. In July 1966, as the SSUFO panel was about to begin its work, the Air Force Foreign Technology Division requested a parallel, in-depth evaluation of about 50 UFO cases for the purpose of "identifying [desirable] changes...in methodology." The investigating group's mandate included an

assessment of "the entire UFO situation." Results of this evaluation of selected cases "did not reveal any evidence of extraterrestrial vehicles, nor anything that might be considered beyond the range of present-day scientific knowledge."

It was also recommended that immediate steps should be taken to "educate the public" about the "sensational but insidious exploitation of UFO reports, by releasing official books, reports, and news items. Also, the extent of public concern and opinion regarding UFOs for use in determining long range requirements should be determined. If results should indicate that public concern has been overestimated, then consideration should be given to dropping all official [government] interest in UFOs."

As it turned out, no steps were taken to "educate the public," but "official interest" would soon evaporate. On August 1, 1969, with the Vietnam War consuming U.S. Air Force time, energy and resources at a voracious rate, General John Dale Ryan became chief of staff. Within a few months, Blue Book was closed. To the Air Force, it seemed that "the UFO phenomenon is mainly that of a public relations problem."

Civilian organizations that purported to take a serious interest in unravelling the UFO mystery were derided. "The fringe of believers in extraterrestrial visitation continues to grow," commented Blue Book in its final report:

UFO hobby clubs are a constant critic of Air Force policies [and] the majority of these clubs profess to be studying the phenomena scientifi-

cally.…However, it should be recognized that the public could be expected to accuse the Air Force of withholding information on UFOs since their investigation has been assigned to Air Force Technical Intelligence. Initial classification of the UFO project and continuous association with the intelligence community has contributed to constant public criticism.…With continued government involvement, the Air Force must announce and maintain a standard policy of releasing information to the public. The public must be continually informed of all matters regarding the UFO phenomena.

On December 17, 1969, Project Blue Book was terminated. Of the total of 10,147 sightings reported to it, 646 remained "unidentified."

The decision to discontinue UFO evaluations was reportedly based on the SSUFO evaluation and a review of the University of Colorado's report by the National Academy of Sciences. The Air Force regulation establishing and controlling the program for investigating and analyzing UFOs was rescinded. Officially, documentation on the former Blue Book evaluation was officially and "permanently" transferred to the Modern Military Branch, National Archives and Records Service. In fact, the documentation was not transferred: all one finds there today are microfilms of the original documentation, whose present whereabouts are unknown.

The U.S. Air Force was officially out of the UFO investigation business.

Overleaf: *A Russian icebreaker in Lancaster Sound, near Baffin Island, at a latitude of 73° north. The crew of a Soviet icebreaker witnessed the remarkable sight of an object smashing through the ice as it flew vertically from beneath the frozen surface of the Arctic Ocean, according to Soviet Navy submarine officer Dr. Vladimir Azhazha.*

Opening the Iron Curtain

During the Cold War era, UFO research was officially frowned upon by the former Soviet Union and almost no information was shared with other countries. By the early 1970s, however, détente had parted the former Iron Curtain, and reports of UFO sightings in the Soviet Union began to reach the West. One of the most bizarre incidents involved Soviet Fighter Pilot (1st Class) Lt. Col. Lev Vyatkin, who told his story years after his experience over Yalta, on the Black Sea, on August 13, 1967.

During a night training flight, Vyatkin saw "a very large oval-shaped object which was somehow fixed to the port of my plane." Advised that no other aircraft were in the area, Vyatkin made a full circle to track the object, which dimmed its lights "as if a rheostat switch had been turned off inside." Then he banked to the left and "saw a flash of bright light from above, straight on the course of my plane. A slanting milky-white ray appeared in front...closing in on the plane.... I hit the ray with the left wing," and the ray "broke into a myriad of tiny sparkles like those you see in a spent firework. The plane shook violently and the instruments read off the scale." Shortly afterward, both the ray and the light above disappeared, and Vyatkin returned to his base safely. However, "for many days afterwards the surface of the wing which had come into contact with the strange ray shone at nights."

According to *The UFO Report*, edited by Timothy Good, an unevaluated CIA report issued the same month as Vyatkin's alleged experience quoted an unidentified Soviet scientist who "emphatically stated that he knew of no sightings of UFOs in the USSR." The CIA report concluded that "The general feeling one gets is that no official treatment of the UFO problem has been given in the USSR."

Ten years later, Soviet Naval Intelligence was taking an active interest in researching "hydrospheric aspects of the UFO issue." According to Dr. Vladimir Azhazha, a Soviet Navy submarine officer in 1977, his research group collected and analyzed many UFO reports, including one from the "floating base" ship *Volga* dated October 1977.

Some 200 miles out from the Kola Peninsula, in the Barents Sea, Captain Tarankin was surprised by a report of helicopters approaching so far from land. But when they reached the ship, everyone realized that they were UFOs. "They were flying around the masts; there were nine in all, and for eighteen minutes while they were flying around the *Volga*, all radio communications were blacked out, and Tarankin was unable to contact the main base to report the event." By the time an Intelligence Service plane arrived to investigate, there was no trace of the mysterious visitors. But Captain Tarankin had ordered his men to draw and photograph the strange objects carefully, "so that when we return to the Soviet Union, no one will be able to say that your captain was drunk or crazy!"

During the ten-year period that Dr. Azhazha's research group was at work (to 1987), their reports to Naval Intelligence were classified "Top Secret." In a 1990 interview in Moscow, Azhazha recalled that "there were too many incidents which could not be denied.... We tried to understand the nature of certain underwater objects that followed our submarines. At times they even anticipated our maneuvers! Initially, we thought they were American devices. One day such an object came to the surface in a rather spectacular fashion. One of our icebreakers was working its way in the Arctic Ocean when a brilliant spherical craft suddenly broke through the ice and flew up vertically, showering the vessel with fragments of ice. All the sailors on deck and the officers on the bridge saw it. And it was hard to deny the hole in the ice!"

In 1979 a group for the study of "anomalous atmospheric phenomena" was established within the USSR Academy of Sciences Institute for the Study of Terrestrial Magnetism and Radioactivity. Dr. Felix Zigel, a professor of cosmology at the Moscow Aviation Institute, and other important Soviet ufologists would contribute to a program that grew steadily in size and scope until about 1990. In 1981 Dr. Zigel stated categorically that "We have seen these UFOs over the USSR; craft of every possible shape: small, big, flattened, spherical. They are able to remain stationary...or to shoot along at 100,000 kilometers per hour...to vanish and reappear at will.... So refined a technology can only be the fruit of an intelligence that in indeed far superior to man."

Astonishing reports continued to emanate from the Soviet Union before its break-up in 1991. They included the account of an Aeroflot TU-134 airliner allegedly escorted by a "yellow star-like object" on a flight between Tbilisi and Tallin (September 7, 1984) and cosmonaut G.M. Manakov's report of a "great silvery sphere" hovering over the Earth on September 27, 1990, as seen from the space station *Mir*.

8: UFO Status
After Blue Book

> **"The fringe of believers in extraterrestrial visitation continues to grow. UFO hobby clubs are a constant critic of Air Force policies [and] the majority of these clubs profess to be studying the phenomena scientifically."**
>
> —U.S. Air Force
> **Project Blue Book final report, December 17, 1969**

The official U.S. government attitude toward UFOs after 1969 reminds one of the mythical king who commanded the ocean waves to stop. They had determined through Project Blue Book, Project White Stork and SSUFO that UFOs were "man-made objects, natural phenomena, or [had a] psychological cause," but this didn't prevent reliable observers from seeing UFOs.

The Sightings Continued

Unidentified objects that defied explanation continued to be observed in the sky. At about 3:00 AM on January 26, 1974, the crew of a Boeing 727 flying near Lisbon, Portugal, observed up to 15 glowing orange objects shaped like saucers moving from south to north in a "precise V formation" above 45,000 feet.

Later that year, a widely reported incident occurred when four Ohio State National Guardsmen aboard a Bell UH-1H helicopter flying near Mansfield,

Ohio, reported sighting a large object on collision course with the UH-1H. The pilot, Captain Coyne, descended, but the object stopped directly in front of the helicopter before continuing westward. After the incident, which was never explained, Coyne discovered that the UH-1H had actually climbed 2,000 feet while adjacent to the UFO.

Air Force personnel, too, continued to see UFOs. On the evening of November 8, 1975, two slow-moving UFOs were observed flying over several of the Strategic Air Command's Minuteman ballistic missile silos in the vicinity of Malmstrom AFB at Great Falls, Montana. The 341st Strategic Air Command post reported that four missile locations reported seeing "a large red-to-orange-to-yellow object." They were being seen about 10 miles south of Moore and 20 miles east of Buffalo, Montana. It was also reported that the Minuteman site at Harlowton, Montana, had observed an object which emitted a light that illumi-

Opposite: *Two days after the sighting of an "egg-shaped" object in Socorro, New Mexico, reported by policeman Lonnie Zamora (left), Major William Connor (center) and Sergeant David Moody investigated the site. Using a Geiger counter to check for radioactivity, they examine vegetation believed to have been burned by exhaust fumes from the UFO. Several major sightings have coincided with unusual radioactivity levels, including the incident at RAF Woodbridge, England, (see page 138).*

nated the site driveway. A security team reported a UFO with white lights, and one red light 50 yards behind a white light. According to the Air Force, between two and seven UFOs were at about 10,000 feet and flying at 18 knots. The command post also reported an "orange-white disk object" 20 miles southeast of Lewistown.

In the pre-dawn hours of September 7, 1976, five "bat-shaped" UFOs were observed near Port Austin, Michigan. They were seen by civilians, as well as police officers and sheriff's deputies, and were also tracked on radar by the U.S. Air Force 754th Radar Squadron at Port Austin. Newspapers in Bad Axe and Saginaw, Michigan, carried accounts of the unusual event.

European sightings attracted greater attention than ever before during the 1970s. "The UFOs exist and, quite evidently, are a matter of the deepest concern to governments of the whole planet" wrote Spanish journalist Juan José Benítez in October 1976. He had just reviewed twelve files full of documentation on UFO reports by the Spanish government, given to him by members of the Air Ministry in Madrid. Only four months earlier, Benítez's newspaper, *La Gaceta del Norte*, had published an interview with General Carlos Castro Cavero, then commanding the Canary Islands air zone, describing the general's own UFO sighting near Zaragoza. He had observed the UFO for more than an hour over the town of Sadaba and reported that "It was an extremely bright object, which remained there stationary for that length of time and then shot off towards Egea de los Caballeros, covering the distance of 20 kilometers in less than 2 seconds. No human device is capable of such speed."

From Italy, in 1978, came six new reports of UFO sightings by military personnel the previous year. Released by the Italian Ministry of Defense, they included an account by two helicopter pilots who had sighted a "luminous circle" over the military airfield at Cagliardi, Sardinia, on October 27th. According to Major Francesco Zoppi and his co-pilot, Lt. Riccardelli, who were on a routine training flight with their squadron, they spotted "an extremely bright orange-colored circle," some 300 meters ahead of them, which was "moving at a speed almost

Below: *These three low-flying UFOs were photographed in Italy, where UFO reports became more frequent during the 1970s.*

identical to our own." The UFO was observed by the second helicopter of their squadron, but not by the third. Reportedly, "the luminous circle then vanished at a speed impossible for any aircraft of this world to equal." It was also observed by control tower personnel, who followed it with binoculars, but "the radar had detected nothing."

After 1969, as European governments began to open their secret UFO files, the lack of official reporting channels left U.S. observers in a quandary. Would UFO reports continue to be taken seriously? With the close of Project Blue Book, trained observers were reluctant to report unusual events and objects because of the implication of mental instability. Pilots were rumored to be pressured into silence, at least on an informal level: No one wants to fly in an airliner piloted by a person who "sees things."

Australia's "UAS" Files
During the 1973 Yom Kippur War in the Middle East, two U.S. servicemen stationed at the U.S. Navy Communications Station at North West Cape, Western Australia, independently reported sighting a mysterious object. According to Royal Australian Air Force files, on October 25 a lieutenant commander, USN—identified only as "M" for security reasons—was driving from the Communications Station to the nearby town of Exmouth, when he saw a large black airborne object about 5 miles (8km) west of him. It hovered at about 2,000 feet (600m) for almost half a minute, then took off to the north "accelerating beyond belief."

The object made no sound and left no exhaust trail.

At about the same time, Fire Captain (USN) "L" was on his way to the base Officer's Club by truck when he saw a large black object resembling a cloud formation hovering in a clear sky. He got out of his vehicle and watched what he described as "this black sphere hovering…completely stationary except for a halo round the center, which appeared to be either revolving or pulsating." He observed it for about four minutes before it took off "at tremendous speed," disappearing within seconds. He estimated that it was 10 meters (30ft) in diameter and hovered over nearby Mt. Athol at 300 meters (985ft).

On October 21, 1978, Air Training Corps pilot Frederick Valentich, 20 years old, became Australia's most notorious UFO witness. He took off from Moorabbin Airport, Melbourne, in a Cessna 182 at 6:19 PM, bound for King Island in Bass Strait, where he was to collect crayfish for the officers of his training corps. The round-trip distance was some 300 miles (500km)—three hours' flying time. Valentich had only been flying for eighteen months and this was his second night flight—unfortunately, it would prove to be his last.

An hour after take-off, Valentich called Melbourne ground control to ask if there were any aircraft in his vicinity below 5,000 feet (1500m). The reply was negative, but Valentich reported that an aircraft with 4 bright lights had just passed above him. Soon after, the voice tape, as transcribed by A.R. Woodward (the full transcript appears in R.F. Haines's

Melbourne Episode), recorded: "Melbourne, it's approaching now from due east towards me." With an increasingly nervous tone, Valentich continued: "It seems to me that he's playing some sort of game—he's flying over me at speeds I could not identify....It's not an aircraft...It's a long shape...it's got a green light and sort of metallic...it's all shiny on the outside."

Valentich then reported that the object vanished, but suddenly he exclaimed: "That strange aircraft is hovering on top of me again....It is hovering and it's not an aircraft." There was a 17-second burst of 'metallic' noise, and no further messages from the Cessna. A search began at 7:29 PM and went on for a week. No trace of Valentich or the aircraft was ever found.

These cases were among the many analyzed in 1980 by Bill Chalker, an industrial chemist who requested access to the RAAF's archives on what were known in Australia as UAS (unusual aerial sightings). The RAAF began to publish summaries of these sightings in 1960 and continued to publish them until 1977, when the number of sightings had diminished considerably. When Chalker asked about the former reports in 1980, he was told that Australia's UFO files were available for inspection, and he undertook an exhaustive review of them. In 1982, the files were made available, in principle, to anyone who wanted to inspect them by Australia's Freedom of Information Act. But two years later, the RAAF stopped taking UFO reports from the public because they have proved not to have "national security significance."

The Kirtland Light

One of the most intriguing UFO events of recent decades reportedly took place during the second week of August in 1980. On August 8, three security policemen assigned to the U.S. Air Force 1608th Security Police Squadron at Kirtland AFB, New Mexico, were on duty inside the Manzano Weapons Storage Area of the Department of Defense Restricted Test Range at Kirtland. The security policemen reported that at 11:50 PM, they observed a very bright light in the sky approximately three miles north-northeast of their position. The light traveled with great speed and stopped suddenly in the sky over Coyote Canyon. They first thought the object was a helicopter. However, after observing the strange stop-and-go aerial maneuvers, they felt a helicopter couldn't have performed in such a way.

Coyote Canyon is part of a large restricted test range used by the Air Force Weapons Laboratory, Sandia Laboratories, Defense Nuclear Agency, and the Department of Energy. Only ground tests—no aerial tests—are conducted in the area.

The light landed in the vicinity of Coyote Canyon, and some time later, the three witnesses saw it take off straight up at a high speed and disappear. Central Security Control (CSC) inside Manzano contacted Sandia Security, a private firm that conducted frequent building checks on two alarmed structures in the area. They said that a patrol was already nearby and would investigate.

Russ Curtiss, of Sandia Security, later reported that at 12:20 AM, on August

9—30 minutes after the sighting—a security guard observed a bright light near the ground, an object he also thought was a helicopter.

After driving closer, he observed a disc-shaped object and attempted to radio for back-up, but his radio did not work. As he approached the object on foot, armed with a shotgun, it took off vertically at a high acceleration. The guard, a former U.S. Army helicopter mechanic, stated with certainty that it was not a helicopter.

On August 10, a New Mexico patrolman sighted an aerial object land in the Manzano area between the cities of Belen and Albuquerque. The patrolman reported the sighting to the Kirtland AFB Command Post, but the Kirtland Public Information office told him that the U.S. Air Force no longer evaluated such sightings unless they occurred on a U.S. Air Force base.

On August 13, the Kirtland AFB Communications Squadron Maintenance Officer reported Radar Approach Control equipment and scanner radar inoperative due to high frequency jamming from an unknown cause. A total blackout of the entire radar approach system—including Albuquerque Airport and all back-up systems—was in effect between 4:30 PM and 10:15 PM. The Defense Nuclear Agency (DNA) Radio Frequency Monitors determined, by vector analysis, that the interference was being sent from an area due east of Radar Approach Control, and northwest of the Coyote Canyon Test Area. After a careful check, it was determined that no tests were being conducted in the canyon area. Base

Security Police conducted a physical check of the area, but because of the mountainous terrain, a thorough check could not be completed by vehicle. A search on foot failed to disclose anything that could have caused the interference. At 10:16 PM, all the radar equipment suddenly returned to normal operation without further incident.

The Air Force investigation concluded that "the presence of hostile intelligence jamming cannot be ruled out....Communication maintenance specialists cannot explain how such interference could cause the radar equipment to become totally inoperative. Neither could they suggest the type or range of the interference signal."

Below: *This strange cluster of unidentified phenomena was recorded on radar at El Toro Marine Corps Air Station in California.*

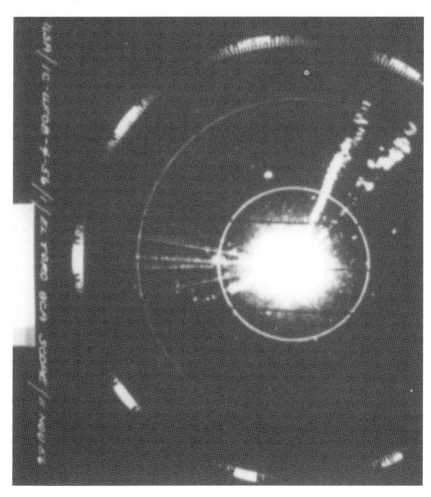

DNA frequency monitors reportedly determined that the interference beam was of a type unknown to their electronic equipment. On August 22, three other security policemen are reported to have observed the same aerial phenomena described by the first three.

The RAF Woodbridge Incident

RAF Woodbridge is a Royal Air Force base located 90 miles northeast of London, and four miles from its sister base, RAF Bentwaters. Activated in 1943, it was closed after World War II, then reactivated in 1952 as a U.S. Air Force fighter base, and turned back to the United Kingdom Ministry of Defence in 1993.

It was reported that at RAF Woodbridge, at approximately 3:00 AM on December 27, 1980, two U.S. Air Force security policemen saw unusual lights near one of the base's gates. Thinking an aircraft might have crashed or been forced down, they requested permission to go outside the gate to investigate. The on-duty flight chief allowed three men to proceed on foot.

They reported seeing a strange, hovering object glowing brightly in the nearby woods. The object was described as metallic in appearance and triangular in shape, six to nine feet across and approximately six feet high. It had a pulsing red light on top, blue lights underneath and was either hovering or on legs. As the men approached the object, it maneuvered through the trees and disappeared. At this time, the animals on a nearby farm went into a frenzy. The object was seen again an hour later.

According to information released in 1983, a daylight survey of the area revealed three depressions, seven inches in diameter, on the ground where the object had been sighted. On December 29, the area was reportedly checked for radiation, and beta/gamma readings of 0.1 milliroentgens were said to have been recorded, with peak readings in the three depressions and near the center of the triangle formed by the depressions. A nearby tree had moderate (.05–.07) readings on the side nearest the depressions.

Later that night, a red, pulsing light was again reported to be moving in the woods near RAF Woodbridge. Reportedly, it broke into five separate white objects, which rose into the sky and were observed moving rapidly and making sharp, angular turns while displaying red, green and blue lights. The objects to the north remained in the sky for an hour or more. The object to the south was visible for two to three hours, and beamed down a stream of light from time to time. Numerous people, including both officers and enlisted men, are reported to have observed the phenomena.

Unexplained Events from the 1980s

In recent years, one of the most amazing series of sightings over the United States is the group known as the Hudson Valley Sightings. The incidents began during the night of July 12, 1984, when a large group of UFOs was observed by many witnesses in the Hudson River valley in New York's Westchester County. There were more than a hundred reports of large, silent, hovering objects with rotating lights. Descriptions came from many highly credible people, including meteorologists, news reporters, police chiefs and off-duty airline pilots. The official explanation was "airplanes in formation," although videos of the objects taken by area residents do not confirm this. Intermittent sightings continued for over a decade.

Pilot sightings during the 1980s included a curious case that occurred over the former Soviet Union on September 7, 1984. A Tupolev Tu-134 jetliner piloted by Captain Igor Cherkashin and copilot Gennadi Lazurin was en route from Tbilisi to Minsk, by way of Rostov, when the flight deck crew observed a yellow, star-shaped object above and to the right, emitting a thin shaft of light toward the ground.

As Lazurin brought this to the attention of the other crew-members, the light became cone-shaped, wider but paler than at first, and the area of the ground that it illuminated was clearly visible. The light then rotated so that it was pointing at the Tu-134. The crew saw a "blinding white point of light surrounded by concentric colored circles" before the light changed to a "green cloud."

The UFO seemed to chase the jetliner at high speed while changing shape. As the Tu-134 came into visual range for the air traffic controllers at the Minsk tower, they, too, could see flashes of light near the aircraft. On the radar scope, meanwhile, the object appeared, disappeared and then reappeared.

One of the most remarkable pilot sightings of the 1980s occurred late on the afternoon of November 17, 1986. Japan Airlines flight 1628, a Boeing 747 with a crew of three, was en route from Iceland to Anchorage, Alaska. At about 6:00 PM, pilot Kenju Terauchi observed white and yellow lights ahead and below to the left of the 747 and assumed it was a U.S. military aircraft. However, the 747's radar indicated a rain cloud rather than a solid object. When the lights followed the jetliner, first officer Takanori Tamefuji contacted the Anchorage Air Traffic Control Center to learn whether there were other aircraft in the vicinity; this was confirmed by radar. The lights began to jump around, and suddenly appeared directly in front of the jetliner.

Near Fairbanks, Terauchi noted an enormous dark object behind the 747, and radioed to ask whether any nearby aircraft could see what he was seeing. A United Airlines jetliner and a U.S. Air Force C-130 were vectored to the area to confirm the sighting, but when they

Below: The UFO in the top right corner of this photograph, taken just north of Kelsey Bay on Vancouver Island, British Columbia, in October 1981, went unnoticed by both Hannah McRoberts, the photographer, and her companions. Not until it was developed did McRoberts realize that she had unknowingly captured a UFO on film.

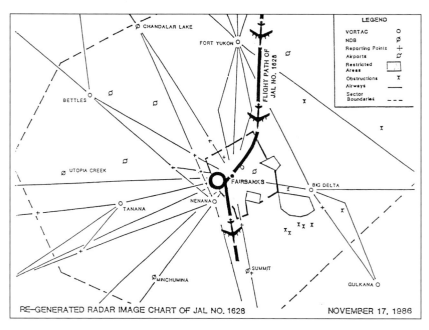

RE-GENERATED RADAR IMAGE CHART OF JAL NO. 1628   NOVEMBER 17, 1986

Above: *The plus signs (+) on this regenerated radar chart of Japan Airlines flight 1628 shows the areas where pilot Kenju Terauchi reported seeing the UFO. Terauchi's repeated alleged sightings of unexplained objects made his claim less believable to investigators.*

arrived, they saw only the Japan Airlines 747. Terauchi reported that the UFO had "disappeared."

It should be noted that Terauchi is said to have reported seeing UFOs on two previous occasions, and he would make a fourth such report in January 1987. He later explained that event, also over Alaska, as city lights reflecting off ice crystals in the clouds. The signal on the 747's radar in the 1986 event could have been reflected by ice crystals, although, unlike rain droplets, they are poor reflectors of radar.

On February 11, 1988, Commandant Simplicio Pinto of Mozambique Airlines was piloting a Boeing 737 on a flight from Quelimane to Maputo, Africa, by way of Beira, when he observed "a wing parachute or something like a flying mattress, that appeared to be in layers. The object had a fluorescent light, like those mercury lamps which give off an intense, very white light."

Radar control at Beira confirmed the existence of an object, which continued to hover above the airport as Pinto made his landing there. After he took off again, Pinto got a better look, and was positive that this object was not an airplane, a balloon, or anything ejected from an aircraft or satellite. He observed three intense lights in triangular configuration emanating from the UFO. Then he switched on two of his landing lights to see if there would be a response. He tried climbing above the object, but as the 737 rose, so did the object, always staying above it. Pinto called in a stewardess to serve as a witness and switched his lights on and off twice. Suddenly, the object rose vertically. As its lights got weaker, Pinto put the jetliner back on its original course.

The object was still in sight as the crew kept in contact with the control tower. The 737 climbed again, but the object remained higher. "By this time we were flying at about 24,000 feet and it seemed stationary," Pinto reported. "I continued to climb, but it appeared to be very far away, even when we reached our cruising altitude of 31,000 feet."

The "Belgian Triangle"

A fascinating seven-month wave of sightings over Belgium began on November 29, 1989, when hundreds of people in the vicinity of Eupen, near Liège, reported seeing a huge triangular UFO with bright spotlights, hovering and overflying the town. One witness described "three powerful searchlights directed to the ground and one orange-red flickering light. As the thing hung in the sky, the searchlights moved across the ground." The reports included visual sightings, both from the ground and in the air, and radar contact by the Bierset Air Force base. An interceptor was sent to investigate the object from the NATO base at nearby Gelsenkirchen, but its pilot could find nothing. During the next few days, witnesses including two policemen reported similar sightings, some of the observers describing colored balls of light descending from the object.

Reports of strange triangular objects began to come in from all over the country: by March 1990, Belgian officials had logged more than 2,500 of them. Sightings were also reported from Germany, notably one in which multiple witnesses observed a large, triangular object with yellow lights at each corner hovering near Coblenz on February 21. Skywatches were organized, and many photographs and videotapes of the UFOs were turned over to the authorities.

The UFO research group SOBEPs, based in Brussels, agreed to co-ordinate these reports, and the Royal Belgian Air Force (RBAF) took charge of tracking and/or intercepting unidentified aircraft. On the night of March 30–31, 1990, a gendarme at Ramillies reported seeing three UFOs showing red, green and yellow lights. At 11:00 PM, police patrols and SOBEPs observers added their report that a single UFO appeared to be flying across Belgium on a steady course. RBAF radars at several sites confirmed these sightings, and two F-16 Fighting Falcons were sent to intercept at 12:05 AM. When their radar locked onto the UFO, which had been flying slowly at 9,000 ft (2750m), it accelerated at an astonishing rate to 970 MPH

(1800km/h) and dived to less than 5,000 ft (1500m). The F-16s gave chase for an hour, with rapid changes of speed and altitude, before returning to their base. At 1:30 AM, observers on the ground reported seeing four UFOs which "lost their luminosity" and "seemed to disappear in four different directions."

Several experts were involved in the investigation of the so-called Belgian triangles, including Auguste Meessen, a professor of physics, and Dr. J.-P. Petit of the French National Center of Scientific Research (CNRS). Their findings, published by SOBEPs in 1991, were roundly criticized by Belgian skeptic Wim van Utrecht, who offered his own analyses the following year.

Van Utrecht pointed out the complete lack of correlation between ground reports and radar read-outs on the sightings of March 30–31 and the disparity between descriptions of the UFOs, ranging from triangular to rectangular, trapezoidal and diamondlike. He speculated that the UFOs reported in November/ December 1989 might have been experimental, self-propelled balloons of triangular shape carrying running lights that conformed to air-safety regulations.

The RBAF, for its part, speculated that the sightings involved USAF "stealth" aircraft, specifically the triangular F-117A fighter, then being tested secretly from bases in the U.K., reportedly over Belgian and German air space. The USAF vehemently denied this on more than one occasion during 1989–90, but, as Peter Brookesmith observed in *UFO: The Government Files* (1996), "there were persistent rumors in aviation cir-

UFOs over France

In France, the Ministry of Defense investigated early UFO reports because of their implications for national security, but shared little information with other countries. One notable sighting had occurred at the time of the Korean wave, early in the morning of June 13, 1952, when a brilliant orange-red light hovered near Le Bourget airport for about an hour, before accelerating rapidly away. Despite the time of night, there were numerous witnesses to this incident, including a pilot approaching the airport and two control tower operators. Another object was observed and tracked by theodolite ten weeks later at a military meteorological station in Villacoublay.

Two French scientists, Aime Michel and René Hardy, investigated and collated many French reports of UFOs, beginning in 1958; they also served as advisors to NICAP. Not until twenty years after the biggest wave of sightings, which had occurred in 1954, did the French minister of defense, M. Robert Galley, reveal that his office had collected a vast number of reports during that crucial year.

These reports were not released, either to the public or to other nations. However, in 1977 the French government created the Study Group on Unidentified Aerospace Phenomena (GEPAN) within the French National Center for Space Studies (CNES). It was designed to be accessible to the public, but, like Project Blue Book, has been accused of dealing only with selected events on a public-relations basis, while referring important sightings and reports to other government agencies. GEPAN is still active, but traditional sighting reports have fallen off since the late 1970s, and public attention has been refocused on the twin hypotheses of alien activity and widespread cover-ups by the authorities.

Perhaps the most startling French report is GEPAN's account of an apparent landing in Trans-en-Provence on February 8, 1981. M. Collini, the witness, was working in his garden when he heard "a low whistling sound" nearby. He turned toward the sound and saw an ovoid object above the trees rapidly approaching the foot of his garden. It touched down behind a small building. M. Collini hurried to the site to look at the object, which rose less than a minute later and moved off, still emitting a low whistle. It left a clear crown-shaped imprint and circular marks on the ground.

Local gendarmes took soil and vegetation samples the following day, and GEPAN investigators took additional samples and interviewed M. Collini on March 20th. The soil samples were determined to have been heated to over 300°C.

cles in the late 1980s that the F-117A was occasionally operating at night from USAF bases in eastern England, while the equally unorthodox-looking B-2 stealth bomber openly visited the U.K....in 1988."

Many experts remain skeptical that the F-117 theory provides a credible explanation of these sightings, however. As a stealth aircraft, the F-117 should have been invisible on radar, yet the Eupen object was seen on radar as far away as the Brussels airport. Further, the objects were observed to hover and move slowly, which would be impossible for any airplane unless it was about to crash. M. Clerebaut, secretary of SOBEPs, believes that the sightings remain unexplained: "We have received reports from pilots, judges, an engineer, a lieutenant-colonel, and a trainee airforce meteorologist—all serious people who saw the thing sometimes from a distance of less than fifty metres."

On October 14, 1990, another mysterious UFO incident occurred near Lostdorf, Switzerland. The sighting began with the observation of two bright white, motionless lights in the sky near the road to Zurich. They were also reported to be large, luminous discs, hovering at different altitudes, but surrounded by a halo or nimbus of light.

As Europe was experiencing a wave of UFO sightings in 1989 and 1990, China experienced several important and unexplained events that also involved glowing objects and lights. On March 18, 1988, Xinjiang Airlines flight 2606 from Beijing came across an odd, round UFO flying in the opposite direc-

tion. It was emitting an intense stream of light. When the crew contacted air traffic control about the light, they were told that no other craft was in their area. After about three minutes, the lighted UFO changed course and flew away. The object was circular on top, and the bottom was "bean" shaped. It was surrounded by a green halo.

Exactly three years later, another Chinese airliner—a British-built Shorts 360 twin turboprop with 36 passengers aboard—was involved in another unexplained UFO incident. An object described as being within a ring of light was observed near the aircraft by an air traffic controller. The object was larger than the aircraft, it had a red light coming from its tail, and its color changed from orange to black. It then was seen to split into two objects, one rectangular and the other circular. They flew back and forth, maintaining a 1,000-foot separation between one another, and then turned and flew quickly toward the plane. Without hitting the aircraft, they joined and flew away.

Below: One theory advanced by the RBAF to explain the wave of sightings over Belgium that began on November 29, 1989, was that triangular-shaped USAF F-117 aircraft were being secretly tested from bases in the United Kingdom. The USAF strongly denied this accusation.

9: The Roswell Revival and Looking Ahead

> **"Since the termination of Project Blue Book, nothing has occurred that would support a resumption of UFO investigations by the Air Force."**
>
> —U.S. Air Force Fact Sheet
> June 1995

The newspapers abruptly stopped reporting the 1947 Roswell Incident when the Air Force officially identified the recovered debris as a weather balloon. Despite unanswered questions and intriguing testimony, the case was ignored by UFO researchers for more than three decades. It is not referred to in the U.S. Air Force evaluations reported in Project Blue Book or its predecessors, Projects Sign and Grudge; nor was it considered in the final report of the Scientific Study of Unidentified Flying Objects (SSUFO). Today, however, the Roswell story has assumed mythical proportions. Rumors of extraterrestrial bodies and government conspiracy abound.

The Forgotten UFO

It has been alleged that the USAAF secured the crash site, recovered wreckage and bodies and took everything to Roswell Army Air Field (RAAF) under extremely tight security for further processing and later exploitation. Reportedly, the USAAF made arrangements on the spot to ship the recovered materials to other bases for analysis. Of the numerous locations mentioned, Wright Field (now Wright-Patterson AFB), Ohio, is the most frequently claimed: it was the home of the Air Technical Intelligence Center and the Air Matériel Command, and thus a logical place to evaluate unknown materials of obscure origin.

It is further claimed that the USAAF covered up all information on the alleged crash and recovery via security oaths to personnel and coercion of others (including alleged death threats). Unsubstantiated stories circulated that an alleged military nurse named Naomi Selff, reportedly an eyewitness to alien bodies at Roswell, was abruptly transferred to London and died in an accident shortly thereafter.

The press conference held by Eighth Air Force commander General Roger Ramey on July 9, 1947, effectively ended Roswell as a UFO-related matter until 1978, when an article appeared in the newspaper *The National Enquirer*. It reported that a former Air Force intelligence officer, Jesse Marcel, claimed to have recovered UFO debris near Roswell

Opposite: Although General Ramey's July 9, 1947, press conference purportedly closed the Roswell case, sightings continued to occur over Roswell, including the glowing object that appeared there on March 21, 1964. Lack of a conclusive explanation and rumors of government conspiracy have kept the Roswell Incident at the forefront of UFO phenomena.

in 1947. A UFO researcher named Stanton Friedman met with Marcel and began to investigate his claims that the material he had handled was from a crashed UFO. Similarly, writers William L. Moore and Charles Berlitz researched and published *The Roswell Incident* (1980), in which they reported interviewing people who claimed to have been at Roswell in 1947 as first- or secondhand witnesses to strange events. Since 1978–80, other UFO researchers, notably Donald Schmitt and Kevin Randle, claim to have located and interviewed new witnesses to unusual happenings at Roswell, including civilians and former military personnel, and more than a dozen books have been published on the subject.

In September 1989 the television program "Unsolved Mysteries" devoted a large portion of one show to a "re-creation" of the supposed Roswell events. The show's invitation to viewers to come forward with further information met with a huge response, which led researchers to many "new witnesses." Fuel was added to the fire of interest in May 1995,

Below: A low-flying, disc-shaped UFO was photographed in August 1988 near the Nevada border just north of "Area 51," the alleged installation in central Nevada that is also known as "Dreamland" and "the Skunk Works."

when Merlin Productions, London, released a film purporting to show an autopsy conducted on one of the "alien bodies" recovered from the spacecraft. The 150-minute "Alien Autopsy," generally judged to be an expensive hoax, was allegedly shot by a U.S. Army photographer named Jack Barnett.

Even before the release of the Merlin film, several major inconsistencies in the new Roswell claims were apparent. For example, it was originally reported that debris had been recovered from a single site; later reports suggested several huge "debris fields." The original description of sticks, paper, tape and metallic-foil debris evolved into rumors of hieroglyphic markings and exotic metal-like materials with extraordinary properties. The 1947 newspaper reports had made no mention of alien bodies, yet new witnesses have come forward testifying to having seen, or heard others report seeing, apparently extraterrestrial creatures at the time of the incident.

A number of the new witnesses interviewed by researchers during the 1980s and '90s were stationed at or lived near Roswell in 1947, and their stories agree in some respects, especially in their claims of a cover-up. Philip J. Corso, who served on the National Security Council at the time, claimed in his book *The Day After Roswell* (1997) that he was involved in the transfer of the recovered debris, and that information relating to the incident was covered up. However, almost all the information supporting an extraterrestrial hypothesis in the Roswell Incident comes from reports made long after the fact, most of them

second- or thirdhand. Kal K. Korff, author of *The Roswell UFO Crash: What They Don't Want You to Know* (1997), cautioned that in most cases, "testimonies from the so-called new witnesses are either overblown and exaggerated by the pro-UFO Roswell authors or they are blatant confabulations."

The Air Force Reopens the Case
After fifteen years of mounting public speculation, the *Washington Post* published an article on January 14, 1994, announcing that New Mexico congressman Steven Schiff would initiate a General Accounting Office effort to "resolve this controversial matter." The director of Security and Special Program Oversight in the office of Secretary of the Air Force, Sheila Widnall, decided that the Air Force should begin to research the Roswell Incident independently, *before* hearing from the GAO.

On February 15, 1994, the GAO notified Secretary of Defense William J. Perry that it would be auditing "the Department of Defense (DOD) policies and procedures for acquiring, classifying, retaining, and disposing of official government documents dealing with weather balloon, aircraft, and similar crash incidents." The bureaucracy's slow wheels began to turn, and the GAO began to locate documents, focusing on the U.S. Air Force files, that would help to establish "the facts involving the reported crash of a UFO in 1949 [*sic*] at Roswell, New Mexico...[and an] alleged DOD cover-up."

While Congressman Schiff's objective was to pierce the cover-up—if one

U.F.O. EVALUATING THE EVIDENCE

existed—the Air Force had a different agenda. It reiterated the truth of its original explanation—that the UFO had been a weather balloon—and its spokesman asserted that it had a "thorough interest" in disproving the charge of a cover-up. Senior Air Force personnel insisted that relevant files should not be "hidden or overlooked," and that the GAO would receive the "best and most complete information available." However, researchers did not go to the U.S. Army for records in such areas as missile launches from White Sands, nor to the Department of Energy to see if its forerunner, the Atomic Energy Commission, had records of nuclear-related incidents occurring at or near Roswell in 1947.

On March 1, a search of both unclassified records and highly classified Air Force records, known as Special Access Programs,

Below: *The perception of the suprisingly humanoid physical structure of extra-terrestrial beings is based primarily on the alleged findings and "alien autopsy" after the 1947 Roswell crash.*

began. If the Air Force had recovered some type of extraterrestrial spacecraft and/or bodies and was exploiting this for scientific and technology purposes, such a study would be operated as a Special Access Program. However, the Air Force categorically denied the existence of such a program of spacecraft or aliens. "Besides the obvious irregularity and illegality of keeping such information from the most senior Air Force officials," said a spokesman, "it would also be illogical, since these officials are responsible for obtaining funding for operations, research, development, and security. Without funding, such a program, operation, or organization could not exist."

The office of the secretary of the Air Force conducted reviews at many military and government locations—for its own investigation and to cooperate with the GAO—including the National Archives and Library of Congress in Washington, D.C., and examined classified files in areas including weapons and missile tests, none of which discussed any activities that could have been misinterpreted as the Roswell Incident. The researchers found only one USAAF document pertaining to UFOs and Roswell in July 1947. This was an entry in the July Historical Report for the 509th Bomb Group and Roswell Army Air Field, which stated: "The Office of Public Information was quite busy during the month answering inquiries on the 'flying disk,' which was reported to be in the possession of the 509th Bomb Group. The object turned out to be a radar tracking balloon."

While the document search was in progress, it was decided to locate and interview several persons who might be able to answer questions generated by the research. This had never been done officially, although most of those contacted reported that they had been contacted before by the media, various writers or other private researchers. To counter possible accusations that those interviewed were still "covering up" because of prior security oaths, the interviewees were provided with authorization to discuss classified information, if applicable, and to override any existing restrictions.

A signed, sworn statement was taken from Lt. Col. Sheridan Cavitt (USAF, Retired), the last living member of the group of three persons known to have been present for the recovery of material from the ranch. Cavitt felt that he had been misrepresented repeatedly by the UFO researchers who had interviewed him, and that his comments were taken out of context so as to change their meaning. He stated unequivocally that the material he recovered consisted of a reflective sort of material like aluminum foil, and some thin, bamboo-like sticks. He thought at the time—and when interviewed in 1994—that what he had found was a weather balloon, and so he had told other researchers.

Cavitt also remembered finding a small "black box" instrument, which he thought at the time was probably a radiosonde. He reviewed the famous photographs of the wreckage taken to Fort Worth (often claimed by UFO researchers to have been replaced by the remnants of a balloon) and identified the materials depicted as consistent with those that he had recovered from the ranch. It is worth pointing out that, while the debris displayed at the 1947 Ramey news conference was alleged to be part of a weather balloon, it was, in fact, that of a RAWIN (Radar Wind) radar target normally suspended from neoprene balloons to measure wind speed by radar.

Cavitt claimed that he had never taken any oath or signed any agreement not to talk about this incident, nor had he been threatened by anyone in the government because of it. He did not even know the incident was perceived as unusual until he was interviewed in the early 1980s.

Also interviewed in 1994 was Major Irving Newton (USAF, Retired), who had been a weather officer assigned to Fort Worth in 1947. On duty when the Roswell debris was sent there, he was sent to General Ramey's office to view the material. In a signed, sworn statement Newton related that he "walked into the General's office where this supposed flying saucer was lying all over the floor. As soon as I saw it, I giggled and asked if that was the flying saucer....I told them that this was a balloon and a RAWIN target."

Newton also stated that: "While I was examining the debris, Major Marcel was picking up pieces of the target sticks and trying to convince me that some notations on the sticks were alien writings. There were figures on the sticks, lavender or pink in color, which appeared to be weather-faded markings, with no rhyme or reason. He did not convince me that these were alien writings."

In conclusion, Newton added that during the ensuing years "I have been interviewed by many authors. I have been quoted and misquoted. The facts remain as indicated above. I was not influenced during the original interview, nor today, to provide anything but what I know to be true, that is, the material I saw in General Ramey's office was the remains of a balloon and a RAWIN target."

The Air Force published their conclusions in July 1994, stating that there was "absolutely no indication that what happened near Roswell in 1947 involved any type of extraterrestrial spacecraft." A similar finding was reported in the GAO audit, published the following year. The Air Force report did not address the subject of alien bodies. It maintained that such claims were frivolous: if witnesses had really seen extraterrestrial bodies, why didn't these enter the Roswell folklore—alongside the "hieroglyphics" and "unknown metals"—until more than 30 years after the crash?

The "Real" Secret: Project Mogul
As early as February 28, 1994, the research team from the office of the Secretary of the Air Force found references to balloon tests at Alamogordo Army Air Field (now Holloman AFB) and at the White Sands Missile Range during June/July 1947. These tests involved "constant level balloons" and meteorological devices used to detect shock waves generated by suspected Soviet nuclear explosions. A 1946 memorandum from Air Matériel Command headquarters described the project and

Right: Highly detailed designs were created to construct the "constant level balloons" used to monitor the status of Soviet nuclear weapons research during Project Mogul, the top-secret program conducted during the sensitive Cold War years. It was later alleged that the Roswell Incident may have involved the recovery of one of these balloon devices.

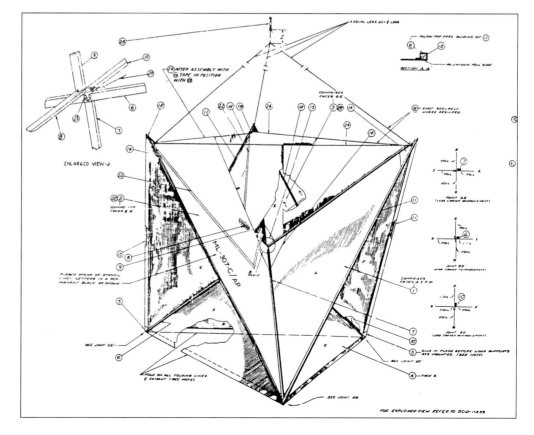

specified that the scientific data be classified Top Secret Priority 1A under the code name Project Mogul.

The purpose of Project Mogul was to determine the state of Soviet nuclear weapons research. Because the Soviet Union's borders were closed during this early Cold War period, the U.S. government sought to develop a long-range nuclear-explosion detection capability. The use of long-range, balloon-borne, low-frequency acoustic detection was proposed to General Carl Spaatz in 1945 by Dr. Maurice Ewing of Columbia University, based on the principle of atmospheric ducting of low-frequency pressure waves, which had been studied as early as 1900.

As part of the 1994 research into Project Mogul, Air Force personnel obtained the original evaluation papers and reports of the project and interviewed members of the original research team, including Dr. Athelstan Spilhaus; the project engineer, Professor Charles Moore; and the military project officer, Colonel Albert Trakowski.

The interviews confirmed that Project Mogul was a sensitive compartmentalized effort. Some of the early developmental radar targets used for tracking the balloons were manufactured by a toy company. No example survives, but the people involved in Mogul recall that these targets were made up of either aluminum foil or foil-backed paper, balsa wood beams coated with white glue to enhance their durability, reinforcing tape, and nylon twine, with brass eyelets and swivels, forming a multi-faced reflector similar in construction to that of a box kite. Some targets were assembled with purplish-pink tape bearing symbols.

The material and the "black box" described by Cavitt were, in Moore's opinion, probably from Flight 4, a "service flight" that included a cylindrical metal AN/CRT-1 Sonabuoy and portions of a weather instrument housed in a box, which was unlike typical cardboard weather radiosondes. A professional journal kept at the time by A.P. Crary, and provided to the Air Force by his widow, showed that Flight 4 was launched on June 4, 1947, but was not recovered. It is quite possible that this Top Secret Flight 4—a balloon train made up of unclassified components—came to rest some miles northwest of Roswell, New Mexico, was shredded by the wind, and was then discovered by rancher Brazel on his property.

As the Air Force conducted this research, it found that several others had realized that the Roswell Incident may have involved the recovery of a Project Mogul balloon device. These persons

Left: *Although no example survives of the balloon devices used during Project Mogul, they were certainly similar to this configuration, which contains 10 conical, polyethylene balloons, a payload and transmitter, radio and antenna and a plastic ballast reservoir.*

The Roswell Report

Headquarters United States Air Force

pices of the Fund for UFO Research (FUFOR), in 1994. Pflock concluded from his research that the Brazel Ranch debris originally reported as a "flying disk" was probably from a Mogul test balloon. However, he believed that a simultaneous incident had occurred nearby, causing the crash of an alien craft from which the USAAF recovered three alien bodies.

The Air Force concluded in their 1994 evaluation that the likeliest source of the wreckage recovered from the Brazel Ranch was one of the Project Mogul balloon trains. Nothing was found "to indicate [that] an official, preplanned cover story was in place to explain an event such as that which ultimately happened."

This conclusion, the Air Force believed, would end the speculation and serve as the final official word on the Roswell Incident—until, during the mounting public interest generated by the 50th anniversary of the incident, the pressure to address the "alien" question prompted the release of a second Air Force study, *The Roswell Report: Case Closed* (U.S. Government Printing Office, June 1997). "I think that with this publication we have reached our goal of a complete and open explanation of the events that occurred in the Southwest many years ago," wrote Sheila Widnall in her foreword. During the few years following the incident, the report explained, the Air Force conducted parachute tests that involved the use of dummies. Hairless, earless, just under four feet tall and with blue "skin," the parachute-test dummies had characteristics that were consistent with descriptions of so-called "alien bodies." When people stumbled upon the

included Professor Charles B. Moore, Robert Todd, and, coincidentally, Karl Pflock—a researcher whose wife is a former staff member of New Mexico Congressman Steven Schiff, who had initiated the GAO evaluation of the Roswell Incident!

A review of FOIA requests revealed that Robert Todd had become aware of Project Mogul several years before and had doggedly obtained a large amount of material on it from the Air Force. Karl Pflock published his own report of the matter, *Roswell in Perspective*, under aus-

crashed test dummies, they probably believed they saw extraterrestrial bodies, and reports to this effect became linked with the Roswell folklore only thirty years later.

Far from closing the case with this convenient revelation of tests that took place after the incident, the failure to produce such an apparently simple explanation during the first round of "exhaustive" research left many skeptics even more convinced of a cover-up.

They're Still out There

During 1995, even as the U.S. Air Force answer to the Roswell Incident was circulating, and the "Alien Autopsy" film was being shown on television, important UFO sightings were occurring. In England, Captain Roger Wills and First Officer Mark Stuart were beginning their descent to Manchester Airport, when a UFO passed under their British Airways Boeing 737. Half a world away, an America West Boeing 757 was pursued by a UFO near Albuquerque in—of all places—New Mexico.

The UFOs are still out there, but trained observers are reticent to report them. They have become the stuff of tabloid journalism, millennial cults and popular fiction, as in such television programs as "The X Files." In the 1990s, UFO reports rarely make the pages of legitimate newspapers; those carried by the tabloids, wherein famous politicians are shaking hands with "aliens," are obvious hoaxes. UFO reports proliferate on the Internet, but many are third- and fourthhand accounts with conflicting information. There are, perhaps, few compelling rea-

sons to report UFOs, but many sound reasons for *not* reporting them. These include apathy, fear of ridicule, lack of knowledge as to where to report and the time and cost of making a report. Back in the 1960s, government investigators discovered that UFO reports are not useful unless they are made promptly. Even so, because of the short duration of most UFO events, the report usually cannot be made until after the UFO has disappeared from view.

Attempts have been made to estimate what fraction of all UFO sightings have been reported. In social conversations many persons describe some remarkable and puzzling thing that they have seen at some time in the past. These sound just as remarkable as many of the cases found in UFO report files, and most of these events go unreported. At the time of the Scientific Study of UFOs (SSUFO) in the late 1960s, only about one person in 10 would report sightings, and that number is probably far less today. For one thing, there is no "official" point of collection for UFO reports as there was when Project Blue Book was active, and for another, UFO observers are less likely to be taken seriously today.

Yet the sightings continue, and, paradoxically, the belief that UFOs are extraterrestrial in origin has become more widespread. A June 1997 poll conducted for *Time* magazine in the buildup to the 50th anniversary of the Roswell Incident found that 22 percent of American adults believe that intelligent beings from other planets have been in contact with human beings. The lack of an official explanation for UFOs has cre-

Opposite: *Released by the United States Air Force in June 1997, The Roswell Report stated that the debris recovered at Roswell in 1947 included human-like dummies that were being used to test a new type of weather balloon. The report claimed that evidence of these test flights had recently been discovered, a statement that seems to support the aura of conspiracy surrounding the Roswell crash.*

ated a void into which any number of strange theories can be dropped—including that of the Heaven's Gate cult, whose members committed mass suicide in the belief that shedding their earthly bodies would facilitate their rendezvous with a UFO in the wake of the Hale-Bopp comet in early 1997.

What does the Future Hold?
In September 1995, Nick Pope of Britain's Ministry of Defence officially stated, "I believe in aliens." A year later, his book, *Open Skies, Closed Minds*, was published. Pope noted that he had been convinced by a number of British sightings which defy explanation. Pope's declaration underscores the general belief that there is substance to the unexplained UFO reports, although the nature of that substance is as elusive for Nick Pope as it was three decades earlier for the U.S. Air Force's Captain Edward Ruppelt. Ruppelt stopped short of accepting the notion of extraterrestrial origin, but astronomer J. Allen Hynek, who had been involved in some UFO research projects, became—like Pope—a believer.

The educated opinions of expert investigators such as Ruppelt, Hynek and Pope are of great value in the evaluation of UFOs. However, barring any irrefutable physical evidence, an explanation for UFOs is unlikely. In 1947, General Nathan Twining noted that "crash-recovered exhibits…would undeniably prove the existence of these objects." He was right, but no one knows whether such exhibits were recovered—or, if they do, they aren't talking.

Does the absence of an official explanation for UFOs mean that *every* sighting can be written off as a weather balloon, a helicopter, an airplane, a hallucination, an optical illusion, or a poorly observed or poorly understood natural phenomenon such as ball lightning, unusually shaped clouds, meteor showers, objects carried aloft by high winds, the planet Venus, luminous swamp gas or fireflies?

There are no concrete facts about the nature of the unexplained UFOs, despite what would seem to be an exhaustive investigation. From 1947 to 1969, the U.S. Air Force evaluated unidentified flying objects under Project Blue Book and its predecessor projects. During this time a reported 12,618 sightings were evaluated, and 701 remained "unidentified." As a result of these evaluations, studies, and experience gained from investigating UFO reports, the Air Force officially concluded that: No UFO reported, investigated and evaluated by the Air Force was ever an indication of a threat to national security; there was no evidence submitted to or discovered by the Air Force that sightings categorized as "unidentified" represented technological developments or principles beyond the range of modern scientific knowledge; and there was no evidence indicating that sightings categorized as "unidentified" were extraterrestrial vehicles.

Having concluded this, the Air Force rescinded its "regulation establishing and controlling the program for investigating and analyzing UFOs." Blue Book documentation was permanently transferred to the Modern Military Branch, National Archives and Records Service.

However, a number of questions remain unanswered. If the conclusions reached by Project Blue Book in 1969 were the same as those reached by its predecessor organizations two decades before, why was Project Blue Book allowed to continue for so many years? Why did the Truman Administration put together a panel to evaluate "the UFO problem" and give it only four days to do its work, work that was finished late on a Saturday night, less than 48 hours before Dwight Eisenhower was sworn in as president? If that group, the Robertson Panel, described UFO reporting as a "morbid national psychology," why did the Air Force continue to collect UFO reports? If Project Mogul could remain secret for many years, why should we believe that news as sensational as an extraterrestrial encounter would be revealed?

Finally, why is it that so many trained observers, over so many years, have continued to see—visually and on radar—apparently solid objects for which there is no explanation? The sheer number of the qualified persons observing these phenomena indicate that there must be something to be observed. Looking to the future, despite the reassurances of governments worldwide, it is likely that next week, somewhere in the world, another UFO will be seen and reported, and official channels will try to craft an evaluation to explain or to discredit the sighting.

As the sightings continue, unofficial speculation has replaced official evaluation, rumors persist and clusters of believers interpret shreds of evidence as confirmed sightings. Take the September 1991 "sighting" during Space Shuttle Mission STS-48. Did a video camera capture an object or objects flying at high speed above the surface of the Earth and into space? Or were they just ice crystals photographed at close range? The official NASA interpretation was that the objects were not vehicles, but some skeptics assume that government denials are really confirmations, and vice versa.

When the "UFO hobbyists" insist that there are alien spaceships at Area 51 at a Nevada Air Force base, and the U.S. government says there is no Area 51, who do we believe? We know that it is official policy to deny that there are bases and fields in the restricted area that is believed to contain Area 51. However, we also know that there actually are bases and fields throughout that area—from Tonopah to Groom Lake and beyond. If the government officially denies one statement that appears to be undeniable, what are we left to believe about others? Likewise, as such related phenomena as crop circles attract the attention of the scientific community—and the public—internationally, are we more prepared to open our minds to the possibility of extraterrestrial UFOs?

In the history of the official evaluation of UFO evidence, numerous government reports have claimed to be the final word on the elusive truth about UFOs. Too often, however, important facets have been ignored, concealed or left unresolved. Thus, the answers left still deeper questions. The final word is yet to be spoken.

Above: An example of a cigar-shaped aircraft—the Northrop X-24B.

phenomena that scientists have recognized only recently are the mysterious "red sprites" and "blue jets." Observed for years by pilots of high-altitude aircraft, and finally videotaped in 1989, they appear above violent thunderstorms as ghostly tongues of light in the mesosphere and thermosphere, 20 miles or more above the surface of the Earth. The blue jets appear as flashes that look like lightning or electrical sparks, while the red sprites can be as tall as 40 miles, often resembling octopi, with many long tentacles. They are rarely seen, but during one 67-minute period in 1994, almost 100 sprites were observed over Colorado and Kansas.

These phenomena might explain some of the sightings that bewildered investigators of the Blue Book era—balls of light that "followed" aircraft before moving rapidly away. Observed and measured, they have yet to be explained. This is also true of the phenomena outlined below, with the theories advanced to account for them.

Technical Analysis

What Are the UFOs?

The most popular current theory is that UFOs are spacecraft piloted by beings from another world. They might also be robot probes, like those we have sent to Venus, Mars and Jupiter. However, at this writing, our only conclusive evidence for extraterrestrial life is the 1996 NASA report of bacteria on the planet Mars.

The reported abilities of UFOs include hovering silently, maneuvering quickly and accelerating instantly to hundreds of miles per hour. No human pilot could withstand such acceleration, nor duplicate the erratic, high-speed maneuvering that has been observed. Dr. Richard F. Haines of NASA infers from these and other characteristics that UFOs may not employ known aerodynamic principles. But what of those sightings that have proved, or may prove, to originate from natural or manmade phenomena? Outlined below are technical considerations that provide background to some of the explanations advanced other than the extraterrestrial theory of UFOs.

Natural Phenomena

Many initially puzzling sightings were later determined to be attributable to natural phenomena, including ball lightning, meteor showers, light refracting through ice crystals, comets and lens-shaped clouds. Among the natural

Manmade Phenomena

During the fifty years and more that UFOs have been systematically evaluated, many sightings have proved to be airborne objects of human manufacture. This category includes weather balloons, disintegrating satellites, unfamiliar aircraft, conventional aircraft distorted by atmospheric phenomena and a variety of new developments in technology in the process of being tested, whether openly or secretly. Given the enormous strides made by science and technology throughout the twentieth century, it is not surprising that untrained observers could identify many or all of these devices as UFOs.

Aircraft Shapes, from Discs to Spheres

In the late 1940s, the disc or circular planform was not known to be in use for either military or civilian aircraft, although intriguing reports of disc-shaped aircraft first emerged during World War II. Small, saucerlike spinning discs were reportedly under development by the

Soviet Union, with the aid of German scientists, in the late 1940s. Modified disc-shaped aircraft, notably the American Vought XF5U-1 "Skimmer," had been test flown.

The disc planform had been avoided because it appeared that the drag induced and the maximum possible lift coefficient, as determined by the Prandtl theory of lift, would be excessively high, since the aspect ratio of a circular planform is low. However, wind tunnel tests of such airfoils indicated much less induced drag increase than expected (though still much larger than conventional aircraft wings), and a high maximum lift coefficient, accompanied by extremely high stalling angles. Thus performance in climb, at altitude, and for long-range conditions would be relatively poor, although high-speed performance would be little affected.

Despite the predicted aerodynamic disadvantages of circular wings, experimental efforts continued. One of the most intriguing results was the Avro Canada VZ-9-AV Avrocar, produced for joint evaluation by the U.S. Army and Air Force, and first tested in 1958. Perfectly disc-shaped, it was powered by vectored-thrust Continental J69 turbojet engines. This vehicle finally took off but, reportedly, it was never able to hover more than a few feet above the ground.

The cigar- or torpedo-shaped body represents an efficient form for the fuselage of an airplane or a missile, but must be launched without lift-providing wings. NASA has tested "lifting body" aircraft, including the Martin X-24A, the Northrop M2 and the Northrop HL-10, but not until long after Project Sign and the early Blue Book era. German experience from the 1940s indicated that the maximum lift might be twice as high as that predicted by the Prandtl theory. Theoretically, a "flying fuselage" could be equipped with extendable wings for takeoff and landing that would be self-contained in flight.

This type of aircraft could also be partially supported at takeoff and landing by the vertical component of the jet thrust. This was

achieved in the British Aerospace/McDonnell Douglas AV-8 Harrier, a vertical takeoff and landing (VTOL) aircraft. An extendable rotor, concealed within the fuselage, could be used as another method for landing and takeoff that would allow wingless flight at very high speed.

Spherical or balloon-shaped objects are inefficient in terms of speed, although balloons do have great range potential. Apart from inflating such vehicles with a lighter-than-air gas, like hydrogen or helium, the sole means of producing lift would be by rotation of the sphere with translational motion relative to the air, or by discharging a stream of air downward—as when air is let out of a toy balloon. Aerodynamic flight could be accomplished with a rotating sphere provided such design problems as stability and control were worked out.

The most common explanation for spherical UFOs is that they are weather balloons, or balloons of other types. However, this does not explain reports that they travel at high speed, or maneuver rapidly. In cases where observers have reported phenomena described as "balls of light," one reasonable explanation is that the lights are suspended from balloons, or that the objects sighted are balloons reflecting sunlight from their surfaces.

Below: First tested in 1958, the saucer-shaped Avro VZ-9-AV was designed in Canada.

Glossary of Terms and Institutions

Air Defense Command/Aerospace Defense Command (ADC): Created in March 1946 as the U.S. Air Force's elite, front-line force to protect American air space from enemy attack, using Fighter Interceptor Squadrons (FIS) and a network of early warning radar sites and stations. It was the primary component of the North American Air Defense Command (NORAD), which included the Royal Canadian Air Force (RCAF). Redesignated the Aerospace Defense Command in 1968, ADC ceased to exist in 1980, when its activities were assigned to the U.S. Air Force Tactical Air Command (TAC).

Air Force Matériel Command (AMC)/Air Force Systems Command (AFSC): The major U.S. Air Force command for providing the resources and personnel to research, acquire and sustain current and future weapons systems, aircraft, avionics and other technology.

Air Technical Intelligence Center (ATIC): The postwar agency of the USAAF/AMC, responsibile for collecting and evaluating intelligence data on foreign aviation and avionic technology, including secret weapons.

Area 51: Allegedly, a secret military facility located on the Nellis AFB gunnery range, south of U.S. Highway 375 in southern Nevada. It has been suggested that the U.S. government has captured extraterrestrial spacecraft and kept their crews, or bodies recovered, in this area since 1947.

Blue Book, Project: The third of three official U.S. Air Force evaluations of UFOs, manned by the Aerial Phenomena Group (APG).

Bogies: A military-pilot designation for unknown aerial objects—usually enemy aircraft—that might pose a threat.

Civil Aeronautics Administration (CAA)/ Federal Aviation Administration (FAA): The U.S. government agency within the Department of Transportation that regulates air commerce and promotes civilian aircraft and airline safety. The CAA became the FAA in 1958.

Delta, Project: A research overview of UFO sightings involving more than one object published by Dr. Richard F. Haines in 1994.

Flying saucer: A generic term coined in 1947 by Kenneth Arnold for a disc-shaped UFO usually characterized by a smooth, metallic surface.

"Foo fighters": Objects observed by combat pilots during World War II and named by a corruption of the Frence *feu* (fire). They were variously described as semi-transparent "crystal" balls emitting red, gold, white, and/or orange hues, or as balls of fire (perhaps ball ligtning) that raced alongside fighter aircraft.

Fund for UFO Research (FUFOR): Study group formed by research physicist Bruce Maccabee in 1979.

GEPAN: French government agency formed in 1977 as the Study Group on Unidentified Aerospace Phenomena.

Ghost rockets: Objects seen in Scandinavia throughout the summer of 1946. There was speculation that they were secret weapons launched by the Soviet Union, which had captured the German A-4 (V-2) test facility at Peenemunde, on the nearby Baltic coast, a year earlier. Explanations ranged from meteor showers to the aurora borealis to postwar hysteria.

Grudge, Project: The second of three official U.S. Air Force evaluations of UFOs, manned by the Air Technical Intelligence Center. Originally known as Project Sign, it was renamed in late 1948 and issued a

single report, dated August 1949, after it had evaluated 244 sightings.

Hangar 13: Allegedly, a hangar located at Wright-Patterson AFB in Ohio wherein the U.S. government concealed captured extraterrestrial spacecraft and/or crews, bodies recovered. Also occasionally called Hangar 18.

"Men in Black": A term coined *c.* 1953 to describe U.S. government agents who allegedly visit the scene of a UFO sighting to "dissuade" witnesses from talking to the press.

Mogul, Project: A Top Secret test project conducted in the late 1940s at New Mexico's Alamogordo Army Air Field (now Holloman AFB) and the U.S. Army White Sands Missile Range. The tests involved a system developed by New York University and Watson Laboratories for using balloons and other meteorological devices to detect shock waves generated by possible Soviet nuclear test devices.

MUFON: Acronym for the Mutual UFO Network, an international investigative group.

National Aeronautics & Space Administration (NASA): A non-military U.S. government agency created in 1958 to manage all American programs directed toward the scientific exploration of outer space and to conduct research into aviation technology. NASA has managed all American manned space missions and probes.

Naval Research Laboratory (NRL): The U.S. Navy's corporate research and development laboratory, created in 1923. It addresses research into the environments of sea, sky and space. NRL is based at Anacostia Naval Air Station in the District of Columbia.

Scientific Advisory Panel on UFOs: A panel established by the U.S. government in 1952 to evaluate Project Blue Book's work in progress. It was known informally as the Robertson Panel, for its chairman.

Scientific Study of Unidentified Flying Objects (SSUFO): A civilian evaluation of UFOs and of Project Blue Book commissioned by the U.S. Air Force in 1966. Also called the Condon Committee.

Sign, Project: The first official U.S. Air Force effort to collect and evaluate UFO reports. It began in January 1948 and ended in February 1949, having evaluated 243 reports.

Sky Hook, Project: A Top Secret U.S. Navy weather balloon program conducted in the United States in the late 1940s.

SOBEPS: Belgian UFO research group that has co-ordinated reports of sightings for the Royal Belgian Air Force.

Radar Wind (RAWIN): A method for measuring wind speed by radar, in which a corner reflector is towed aloft by a neoprene balloon. RAWIN was used in Project Mogul during the late 1940s.

UAS: Australian Air Force term for "unusual aerial sightings."

Unidentified Flying Object (UFO): An object or phenomenon reported to have been seen or tracked in the sky that cannot be explained by known natural or manmade phenomena.

White Stork, Project: An in-depth evaluation of 50 UFO cases, conducted in 1966 by the U.S. Air Force Foreign Technology Division. Its purpose was "identifying procedural changes that should be made in Blue Book methodology" and, more generally, assessing "the entire UFO situation."

Index